COWBOYS & ALIENS™

COWBOYS & ALIENS™

The Illustrated Screenplay

Screenplay by Roberto Orci & Alex Kurtzman & Damon Lindelof
and Mark Fergus & Hawk Ostby. Screen Story by Mark Fergus
& Hawk Ostby and Steve Oedekerk. Based on Platinum Studios'
"Cowboys and Aliens" by Scott Mitchell Rosenberg.

INSIGHT 👁 EDITIONS

San Rafael, California

INSIGHT ⬥ EDITIONS

P.O. Box 3088
San Rafael, CA 94912

www.insighteditions.com

Library of Congress Cataloging-in-Publication Data available.

ISBN: 978-1-60887-025-7

ROOTS of PEACE   ⊕ REPLANTED PAPER

Insight Editions, in association with Roots of Peace, will plant two trees for each tree used in the manufacturing of this book. Roots of Peace is an internationally renowned humanitarian organization dedicated to eradicating land mines worldwide and converting war-torn lands into productive farms and wildlife habitats. Together, we will plant two million fruit and nut trees in Afghanistan and provide farmers there with the skills and support necessary for sustainable land use.

Manufactured in Canada

10 9 8 7 6 5 4 3 2 1

Designed by Tim Palin

Cowboys & Aliens

COWBOYS

&

ALIENS™

The Illustrated Screenplay

FADE UP ON:

An EYEBALL in MACRO -- quickly dilates -- the frame pops out of focus -- blurred images -- flash frames -- NIGHTMARISH:

TERRIFYING DEVICES (LASER SCALPEL) -- SILHOUETTES -- creatures? -- WE'RE RUNNING THROUGH DARK CAVERNS -- HORRIFIC SCREAMS -- ZOMBIE-LIKE HUMAN FACES STARING UP AT WHAT LOOKS LIKE A GLOWING COCOON -- SOME KIND OF BIOLUMINESCENT GOO INSIDE FLASHING AT STACCATO, SEIZURE-INDUCING INTENSITY -- NOW WE'RE RUNNING TOWARD SUNLIGHT BLASTING FROM A CAVERN EXIT IN THE DISTANCE, AS WE REACH IT WE WHITEWASH TO:

EXT. NEW MEXICO DESERT - DAY

The BLAZING SUN as -- A MAN SITS UPRIGHT, GASPING, TRYING TO SCREAM! No sound comes. He has no voice. Parched. He's handsome . . . but hard. We'll call him THE MAN IN BLACK; the color of his dirty clothes. He looks around, taking in his surroundings:

WIDE: He's a small speck in the BARREN DESERT. How did he get here? And where the hell is here?

Coughing, the man painfully forces himself up. His shirt's torn open, and . . . OWW. A WOUND in his side. He touches it, winces. No memory of that either. Something glints on his wrist:

A STEEL BRACELET. No clasp to pull it off. Strange DIVOTS crisscross in the gleaming steel. The man reaches into his pocket, feeling something. Pulls out:

A WORN PHOTOGRAPH OF A WOMAN. Young, beautiful. Smiling. He stares: Does he KNOW this woman? Is this even HIS hat?

The Man grabs a ROCK, begins to hammer at the bracelet on his arm. No use. It's strong as hell. A RUMBLE catches his attention -- he turns -- quick -- hand reaching towards his hip on instinct, but there's no holster. NO GUNS.

THREE RIDERS ON HORSEBACK are coming over the rise, followed by their DOG. These are the CLAIBORNE BROTHERS and their

FATHER -- WES (Daddy), MOSE, and LUKE. Dusty and tough. Wes gallops right up to our Man, gives him the once over --

                    WES CLAIBORNE
          We're riding toward Absolution. You know
          how far west we are?

The Man's got no idea what he's talking about.

                    LUKE CLAIBORNE
          Maybe he's a dummy.

Wes hops off his horse, right in The Man's face now --

                    MOSE CLAIBORNE
          Some reason you don't wanna answer my
          question, friend?

And now, Mose nods to the BRACELET on The Man's wrist --

                    WES CLAIBORNE
          Look, there, he's carryin' iron on his
          wrist . . . and he's been shot.

Luke spurs his horse behind him -- The Man's SURROUNDED.

                    LUKE CLAIBORNE
          Could be he's done broke out of the
          hoosegow -- might well be bounty money.

Wes nods as he slides a SAWED-OFF SHOTGUN from his back scabbard. Cocks it. The dog growls --

                    WES CLAIBORNE
          Not your lucky day, stranger. Turn real
          slow now and start walking.

But The Man doesn't move. The Claibornes share glances. Wes steps forward -- raising his rifle -- the dog growls LOUDER, feeling the danger --

                    WES CLAIBORNE (CONT'D)
          I said high-heel it, or --

THE MAN MOVES RATTLESNAKE FAST -- yanks the shotgun forward as **BLAM!** -- shot goes WILD -- suddenly the gun's in THE MAN'S HANDS -- **BLAM!** Wes is blown backward, HOLE IN HIS CHEST!

As Mose draws his pistol, The Man FLIPS the rifle again -- **BLAM!** MOSE FLIES OFF HIS SADDLE as The Man rolls -- UNDER Luke's horse -- grabbing Luke's ankle -- suddenly Luke's FLAT on his back -- breathless, staring UP at the barrel:

LUKE CLAIBORNE

-- P-please, God -- <u>d-don't</u> --

The Man PULLS the trigger, but CLICK! <u>The rifle's EMPTY</u>. Luke's relief is short as The Man SLAMS the gun butt down, knocking him out cold. And all of this took about ten seconds. <u>The Man in Black is a cold-blooded KILLER</u>. But somehow . . . he didn't seem to KNOW it. Confusion. He drops the rifle, looks down at his hands . . . <u>covered in BLOOD</u>. And the bodies in his wake. The dog looks calm now, recognizing its new master.

<u>JUMPCUTS</u> -- The man, pulling CLOTHES off the men's bodies -- strips off his bloody shirt -- grabs a new one, blood starts seeping through -- a JACKET to cover that up -- sorts through pockets -- finds CASH.

Pulls a PISTOL from a holster, feels the weight and grip, cocks the pistol, spins the barrel and listens to the ease of the cylinder spin: not fast enough. Tosses it aside. Does the same with another: nope. Then the next: <u>yes</u>.

Snaps the holster off the body, slings it on, jams the gun in. Sees a DARK HAT. Slips it on. Perfect fit. And with a WHACK, The Man sends two horses galloping, mounts the third, wincing. Starts to trot . . . sees the dog following . . .

THE MAN IN BLACK

Get outta here. Leave me alone.

But the dog keeps following. Like they're friends now. The man turns away dismissively as we BOOM UP to reveal the WIDE-OPEN VALLEY below . . . and a row of BUILDINGS within it:

EXT. TOWN - BEHIND MAIN STREET - DAY

The Man rides in and we follow him toward a dying hamlet, once prosperous. Behind the row of buildings, The Man slips around back to avoid being seen -- finds an open door -- quickly enters:

INT. BACK ROOM - DAY

Not sure where we are. The Man looks back at the dog --

> **THE MAN IN BLACK**
> Stay.

It sits by the door as The Man enters, guarded --

> **THE MAN IN BLACK (CONT'D)**
> -- Hello?

Nothing. Into a small kitchen area -- bottle of whiskey -- uncorks it with his teeth -- drinks -- pours some on the wound -- then A RIFLE COCKS behind him:

Meet MEACHAM, the town preacher. A tough, wash-foot Baptist:

> **MEACHAM**
> Palms to heaven, friend.

The Man turns up his hands. Meacham approaches cautiously, pressing his rifle to The Man's neck as he removes the PISTOL from The Man's holster. Or, we should say, as The Man lets him . . .

> **MEACHAM (CONT'D)**
> Turn around.

As he does, Meacham sees the blood pooling through his shirt:

> **THE MAN IN BLACK**
> Been shot.

> **MEACHAM**
> Only two kinds of men get shot --
> criminals and victims.

(tosses the gun aside)
Well? Which one <u>are</u> you?

                    THE MAN IN BLACK
        . . . I don't know.

Meacham hears the HONESTY in his voice. Knows a lost soul
when he sees one.

                        MEACHAM
        Got a name, Brother?

                    THE MAN IN BLACK
        Don't know that either.

                        MEACHAM
        What <u>do</u> you know?

                    THE MAN IN BLACK
        . . . English.

Off Meacham, intrigued -- we CUT TO:

INT. CHURCH - LATER - DAY

The Man steps through swinging doors, hands still up, with
Meacham behind him, still holding a rifle:

                        MEACHAM
        Take a seat.

                    THE MAN IN BLACK
        This your place?

                        MEACHAM
        Six days a week it is. On the seventh, it
        belongs to the Lord.

Ah, we're in a CHURCH. The Man sits among the makeshift
pews.

                    MEACHAM (CONT'D)
        Where'd you ride in from?

                    THE MAN IN BLACK
        . . . West.

                    MEACHAM

          That's a big place . . . West.

Meacham, sizing The Man up, starts to let his guard down.
The Man's face registers the sound of Meacham putting his
rifle down as he moves to a corner and grabs a MED-KIT.

                THE MAN IN BLACK

          Woke up in the desert. Like I dropped out
          of the sky.

                    MEACHAM

          Well, now, I certainly recall one such
          story happening before . . . fella by the
          name of Lucifer.
                    (beat)
          Come into the light.

ECU: A match ignites a KEROSENE LAMP. Now Meacham runs a
NEEDLE under the LAMP FLAME; gestures to a table: Sit.
The Man lays across it, pulls up his shirt, revealing the
wound --

                MEACHAM (CONT'D)
          Try'n hold still . . .

Meacham pokes the hot needle through the wound -- The Man
winces slightly, bearing it stoically. Through the pain:

                THE MAN IN BLACK

          . . . mining town?

                    MEACHAM

          Yeah, but no gold. Most everyone moved
          on to new diggings in the Mimbres Range.
                    (studies the wound)
          Odd wound. Looks . . . cauterized.
                    (beat)
          This isn't a gunshot. Where'd you get it?
                    (The Man stares)
          Right: You don't remember. Well, I can't
          absolve you for your sins if you don't
          recall 'em. That bein' said . . .

Meacham looks up, eyes twinkling. This is not a fire n' brimstone preacher. This is a guy who GETS IT --

                    MEACHAM (CONT'D)
          Whether you end up in heaven or hell . .
          . it's not God's plan . . . it's yours.
                    (beat)
          You just gotta find out what it is.
                    (pulls the thread; finishes stitching)
          Finger?

The Man obliges, holding the knot with his index finger as Meacham ties it off, admiring his work:

                    MEACHAM (CONT'D)
          Not too b --

SMASH!!! The window EXPLODES as a BULLET rips through. WHOOPS and HOLLERS outside! Meacham peers out the door --

                    MEACHAM (CONT'D)
          Damn Dolarhyde kid, drunk again --

He heads out toward the melee. Off The Man, eyes narrow --

EXT. ABSOLUTION - MAIN DRAG - OUTSIDE SALOON - DAY

Meet PERCY DOLARHYDE, a drunk, cocky, hot-tempered bastard -- shooting off his pistol into the GOLD LEAF SALOON SIGN above the bar. His ENTOURAGE watches, amused; only one of the men isn't smiling -- stone-faced NAT COLORADO, half-Apache, tough as hell, with a sadness behind his eyes -- as saloon owner CHARLES "DOC" SORENSON, wearing glasses and an apron, BURSTS through the swinging saloon doors --

And all of what follows, we note, is observed by a mysterious SILHOUETTED FIGURE in an alleyway --

                         DOC
          Hey hey, Percy, what're you doin'?!!

PERCY

Little target practice, Doc! Don't worry,
ain't gonna wrinkle your dress --

BLAM! Percy fires into the sign again, as Doc's wife MARIA
rushes out urgently, trying to get Doc out of harm's way --

DOC	MARIA
STOP! There's roomers upstairs!	-- it's okay, there's no one upstairs --
-- Maria, please, go back inside --	-- Mira, he's drunk, just let him be --
-- bad enough he drinks for free, now he's gotta shoot up the place?!	

Percy WHIRLS on Doc -- wild-eyed -- gets in his face:

PERCY

What was that, Doc? What'd'ya say?

MARIA
(forcing a smile)
He didn't say anything. Por favor, patron,
what else can I get you and your men?

PERCY

No, no . . . I wanna hear what you said.
You ungrateful for our business? Wasn't
for my daddy's cattle, there'd be no coin
goin' through this town! No meat on your
tables, your doors'd be closed!

DOC

Don't mean no disrespect to your father,
Percy, you know that --

-- but Percy KNOCKS Doc's glasses off his face -- they
HIT the ground. Humiliation and anger growing, Doc kneels
to pick them up . . . as Percy LAUGHS and pulls his gun
again, kicks up dust, FIRES into the ground beside Doc,
who recoils:

                         PERCY
          You see his face? He thought I was about
          to blow his head off!

Now Meacham steps in, helps Doc find his glasses and get
up:

                        MEACHAM
          All right now, Percy, these people are
          scared enough of the damn Apaches without
          you shootin' your gun off.

                         PERCY
          Know what, Preacher? You just gave me an
          idea. I know it ain't Sunday, but what
          say we take up a collection for the poor
          man --

He takes his own hat off head, turns it out like a beggar,
swings his GUN menacingly at the townsfolk:

                     PERCY (CONT'D)
          Who's got money? Greenbacks or silver, we
          won't pay no mind!

At gunpoint, they DO. These poor folks start tossing change
in Percy's hat:

                     PERCY (CONT'D)
          Much obliged . . . Much obliged . . .
          Mighty Christian of ya . . . I'm sorry
          Doc's bad luck has to be taken out on you
          good people . . .

Now he sees someone who isn't chipping in: OUR STRANGER,
watching from the corner steps.

                     PERCY (CONT'D)
          Hey, you, too.

But The Man doesn't move. Percy MOVES toward him and swings
the gun up in his face. Still, The Man doesn't flinch,
eerily calm:

THE MAN IN BLACK

Watch where you point that thing. Before
you get hurt.

ON NAT. Something about this man. Something FAMILIAR.
Whatever it is, it's lost on Percy, who's riled; moves
close to The Man's ear -- whispers menacingly:

PERCY

I'm gonna give you the benefit of the
doubt, 'cause maybe you don't know who I
am, but I --

THE MAN'S KNEE SHOOTS UP INTO PERCY'S BALLS. Percy doubles
over, eyes bulging, GASPING. Without a word, The Man walks
away. A FEW DEPUTIES, including one we'll call DEPUTY
DUFFY, linger to their left as Percy whirls, aiming at The
Man's back:

PERCY (CONT'D)

HEY! YOU! TURN AROUND!

But The Man just keeps walking, enraging Percy even more:

PERCY (CONT'D)

HEY: I'M TALKING TO YOU!

He fires a warning shot to the left -- ACCIDENTALLY WINGING
DEPUTY DUFFY IN THE SHOULDER, ON THE PORCH. Meacham rushes
to help Deputy Duffy as Percy, stunned, stammers back:

PERCY (CONT'D)

Whoa! Where the hell'd he come from?!

SHERIFF JOHN TAGGART, 50's, and Deputy CHARLIE LYLE,
carrying a shotgun, come RIDING INTO TOWN. Both dismount.
Taggart sees Duffy's been shot; Taggart's grandson, EMMETT,
scuttles in to greet him:

SHERIFF TAGGART

You go tie up the horses, alright?
        (as Emmett leads the horses off)
What happened here?!

PERCY

It -- it was a warning shot! It wasn't my
fault! He came outta nowhere!
        (swings gun at The Man)
        (re: The Man)
He dry-gulched me! Try and make me look
like a fool!

Taggart glances at The Man, a new stranger in town --

SHERIFF TAGGART

You crossed a line, Percy. You went and
shot a deputy. I gotta lock you up.

ON COLORADO. Protectively, his hand lingers over his gun
handle -- to Taggart:

NAT COLORADO

You know that's not a good idea.

SHERIFF TAGGART

Nat, you know he drew blood on a lawman.
I don't have a choice -- you get your
crew outta here, now.

Colorado -- DECISION -- sensibly nods and starts to go:

PERCY

You sonofabitch! Don't even THINK about
leavin' me!

NAT COLORADO

I'll tell your father what happened
today.

Taggart watches Colorado and the men RIDE OFF. Shit, that'll
bring more trouble. Percy, scared, finally drops the gun
as Deputy Lyle hauls him off to the jailhouse. The other
deputies help up Deputy Duffy, bleeding --

PERCY

It was an accident!

Taggart looks to The Man, offers a hand:

SHERIFF TAGGART
Kyle Taggart.

The Man shakes, saying nothing. His bracelet GLINTS --
and we go back to that SILHOUETTED FIGURE in the alley,
stepping forward now:

A WOMAN -- Not the same woman we saw in the photo. A
heart-stopping beauty. She sees the bracelet and seems
to RECOGNIZE IT, as -- Jake starts to go. Dog follows.
Taggart's bothered by something:

SHERIFF TAGGART (CONT'D)
Hey, Mister, I know you from somewhere?

THE MAN IN BLACK
(beat: Does he?)
. . . couldn't say.

Off he goes. Taggart lingers a beat before moving quickly
back to the office. The WOMAN takes frame, starts FOLLOWING
The Man discreetly . . . eyes crackling with heat-seeker
focus . . .

EXT. CATTLE RANGE - DUSK

30 head of CATTLE. Three COW HANDS eat by a fire: ED,
LITTLE MICKEY, and ROY MURPHY, drunk, slugging a bottle .
. .

ED
Take it easy on that Taos Lightning,
Murphy -- Mr. Dolarhyde don't like
drinkin' on the job.

ROY MURPHY
Don't give a rat's ass what the high-and-
mighty Colonel don't like. Don't care how
many Indians he sent under, neither.

LITTLE MICKEY
You sure flap them gums a lot when the
boss ain't around.

ROY MURPHY

                I'd say it if he was here! Money makes
                you soft, Boys . . . take it from me.

Murphy lets out a big BURP, tosses the whiskey bottle -- it
SMASHES against a rock.

He stumbles drunkenly down an embankment to relieve himself
in a river. We TRAVEL with him, away from the men. Wobbling,
he drops his shorts and lowers himself over the water . . .
then:

KA-BWHAAAM! A MASSIVE SONIC BOOM SENDS A SHOCKWAVE STRONG
ENOUGH TO KNOCK ROY MURPHY OFF HIS FEET AND INTO THE WATER!

WE GO UNDERNEATH THE SURFACE WITH HIM -- BUBBLES --
CONFUSION -- AS HE BREAKS THE SURFACE, THE SOUNDS HE HEARS
SHOCK US:

EXPLOSIONS, LIKE AN ATTACK FROM ABOVE -- THE MEN SCREAMING
OVER THE HILL, COWS BLEATING -- THEN -- WHOOOSH! INDISTINCT
OBJECTS CREST THE HILL AND ROCKET BY OVERHEAD -- WATER
ROOSTERTAILS AS THEY STREAK OVER, LIKE A JET SKIMMING WATER
--

ROY SCREAMS, DUNKS BACK UNDER THE SURFACE AS THE OBJECTS
PASS -- GONE AS FAST AS THEY CAME.

ON THE SHORE -- A terrified Roy crawls back. Coughing,
staggering up to realize a tree is ON FIRE. Stumbles up
the embankment . . .

SHOCK. As we PULL BACK to reveal . . . a BURNED COW
CARCASS. Then another. Four or five of them. The rest of
the cows, the ones that survived, are RUNNING OFF into the
field.

(*NOTE -- WHEN WE SEE THE TOWN ATTACK, WE WILL UNDERSTAND
THAT SOME OF THE CATTLE WERE TAKEN AND SOME WERE INCINERATED
BY LASER FIRE.)

CAMERA RISES ON A CRANE to reveal Roy standing amid the
now-empty field . . . and the other men are GONE. A WAILING
SCREAM takes us to --

INT. SHERIFF TAGGART'S OFFICE - DUSK

Deputy Duffy, in pain, sits at Taggart's desk as Deputy Lyle dresses his bloody shoulder.

                    DEPUTY LYLE
          Hold still, dammit, hold still --

PERCY, locked in a cell across the office. Sobering up but still drunk:

                    PERCY
          You know this is all your fault? Lettin'
          that stranger dry-gulch me --

                    DEPUTY DUFFY
               (as Lyle tightens the bandage)
          AAARGHHH! STOOOOP!!!

Now, TAGGART TAKES FRAME, pulling shotguns off the rack, hands them to the rest of the deputies --

                    PERCY
          Why don't you do yourself a favor and
          lemme go right now, we'll say this never
          happened . . .

                    SHERIFF TAGGART
          But it did happen.
               (low, to Deputy Lyle)
          Where's the wagon?

                    DEPUTY LYLE
          On its way --

                    SHERIFF TAGGART
          We gotta get him out of here fast.

                    PERCY
          What wagon?
               (beat)
          WHAT WAGON?!

                    SHERIFF TAGGART
          Federal marshal's bringing you to Santa Fe.

                              PERCY

          <u>Federal Marshal</u>?! You done lost your
          mind? It ain't like I'm Billy the Kid!!
          This might'a just cost you your miserable
          <u>life</u>. My daddy hears you put me in an
          iron coach, he'll kill ya --

                          SHERIFF TAGGART

          Percy, you wounded an officer of the law.
          I don't have to --

Suddenly, he STOPS. Something's caught his eye on the
posting board. He YANKS a piece of paper off the wall,
speechless.

                              PERCY

          But he's fine! He's all fixed up! My
          balls hurt worse than his shoulder!

                          SHERIFF TAGGART
                     (sotto; to himself)
          Sonofabitch . . .

WHAT DOES HE SEE? Before we get a chance to KNOW --

INT. GOLD LEAF SALOON - DUSK

Doc stews silently as he serves a couple of beers to
patrons at a table -- they CHUCKLE, making fun of him:

                          SALOON PATRON

          Can you put that on Percy's tab?

                              DOC

          Very funny. Fifty cents.

Maria reads her his frustration, quietly intercedes:

                              MARIA

          I can take over, *mi amor*. Why don't you
          rest . . .?

                              DOC

          We got customers. I don't need any rest.
          What're you sayin'?

          MARIA   DOC

Nothing . . . just that   They made a fool out of
I --   me -- you don't have
                              to dress it up. Now
                              these people got less
                              confidence in me -- in
                              this establishment --

                             MARIA

          That's not true, I just didn't want you
          to get shot --

                              DOC

          Well, I'm fine --

                             MARIA
                    (quietly)
          Maybe we don't belong here.

He looks at her, male-pride, wounded anger blocking his
ears from hearing what she's really saying:

                              DOC

          You wanna leave?

                             MARIA

          How can you think that? I followed you
          here because I'd follow you anywhere.
          Esto es tu sueno, your dream. Remember
          how happy we were when we first came?

She moves closer, trying to reach him . . . but her every
loving gesture adds injury to Doc's feeling of impotence:

                              DOC

          Don't you understand? I can't protect
          you. Can't even protect myself . . .

                             MARIA

          You don't have to prove anything. You're
          the bravest man I know.

She tries to kiss him, but he PUSHES her away --

                         DOC
          I'm not a child.

He heads upstairs. Angry at her, himself, the world. Her
eyes: wounded. But she covers instantly, turning back to
her patrons at the bar with a smile as . . .

THE MAN enters with the dog. Passes a window, where EMMETT'S
FACE rises up, peering in as The Man sits at the bar, the
dog heeling at his feet.

                    THE MAN IN BLACK
          Steak. Whiskey.

Maria uncorks a bottle of rye, pours him a shot:

                        MARIA
          I have a nice *Pasole* today. On the house.
          For what you did.

She leaves the bottle. He throws back the shot and stares
at his strange BRACELET -- a thousand unanswered questions
in his eyes. Senses a PRESENCE beside him, turns . . .

THE WOMAN FROM THE STREET is sitting there. Just . . .
staring at him. Eye-lock. Immediate CHARGE. But it's an
odd beginning . . .

                    THE MAN IN BLACK
          I know you?

The dog gives a little WHINE and LICKS her fingers . . .

                        ELLA
          No. But your dog likes me.

He turns away, pours himself another shot:

                    THE MAN IN BLACK
          You can have him.

                        ELLA
                (beat; his eyes narrow)
          My name's Ella.

He doesn't offer his name. Just stares. Her eyes go to his wrist . . .

                    ELLA (CONT'D)
          I like your bracelet.

She reaches out . . . and TOUCHES it. He lets her for a beat, reading her strange intensity, before he moves his arm away.

                THE MAN IN BLACK
          There something you know about me, Lady?

She just looks back at him. INTO him. Realizing:

                    ELLA
          You don't remember anything . . .

This is getting real weird:

                THE MAN IN BLACK
          What do you want?

                    ELLA
          I know you're looking for something.
                (beat)
          So am I.

Their faces CLOSE. But man, she's UNNERVING. He throws back another shot, grabs his hat:

                THE MAN IN BLACK
          Well, good luck to you.

Starts walking away, toward the exit. She's off the stool to follow but suddenly the batwing doors SWING OPEN and SHERIFF TAGGART enters, along with Deputy Duffy, Deputy Lyle, and 2 other Deputies carrying rifles. The Man STOPS, sensing trouble. The lawmen treat him like he's a powder keg about to go off . . .

                SHERIFF TAGGART
          Mind following me down to the office so
          we can have us a chat, Fella?

THE MAN IN BLACK
No need. Moving on.

SHERIFF TAGGART
Well, I'm gonna need you to come with me
all the same.

Duffy has a shotgun in his right hand, his left shoulder
wounded from the gunshot.

ON ELLA -- Behind them, we follow her HAND as it, too,
slips down toward her gun handle. What's she about to do?
As slowly, she moves closer in behind The Man . . .

ONE OF THE YOUNG DEPUTIES

Cocks the rifle. The Man stares him down, low:

THE MAN IN BLACK
Wouldn't do that.

The young Deputy blanches under his stare . . . as Duffy
raises his shotgun in his right hand -- The Man then grabs
the rifle from Deputy Lyle, who's closest to him, CHUCKS
it, PULLS him closer, SLAMS his head down on the table as
The Man pulls his own gun -- SHOOTS DUFFY IN THE LEG --
PUNCHES the third Deputy's THROAT, SLAMS him into a bench
-- The FOURTH straight down on the Faro table --

TAGGART levels his REPEATER -- but The Man just GRABS the
barrel as Taggart FIRES a round into the ceiling -- now the
rifle's in THE MAN'S HANDS and just before he PULLS THE
TRIGGER on Taggart:

EMMETT
NO!!!!!

The Man SNAPS over to see EMMETT AT THE WINDOW. About to
watch his grandfather's MURDER . . . and The Man lowers
the gun:

THE MAN IN BLACK
I told you, I don't wanna hurt anyb --

CRACK! The butt of a PISTOL WHIPS the side of his skull! The Man DROPS as we REVEAL who just knocked his ass out:

ELLA! Taggart draws a gun and pins The Man, whipping out that piece of paper he pulled from his office . . .

> ### SHERIFF TAGGART
> Yup -- that's him.

NOW WE SEE, IT'S A WANTED POSTER WITH THE MAN'S FACE ON IT:

> ### SHERIFF TAGGART (CONT'D)
> "Jake Lonergan. Wanted Dead or Alive."

And The Man . . . now forever known as JAKE . . . stares WOOZILY into his OVERTURNED HAT . . . the photo tucked inside of the BEAUTIFUL WOMAN . . . her image goes BLURRY . . . then BLACK:

INT. CABIN/CAVERN

Unclear where we are -- A WOMAN'S FACE -- THE WOMAN FROM JAKE'S PHOTOGRAPH -- she SCREAMS in terror --

INT. JAIL CELL - NIGHT

JAKE'S EYES SNAP OPEN OFF THE SCREAM. His POV: A FACE comes into FOCUS -- PERCY. GRINNING from the next cell:

> ### PERCY
> You're gonna burn, Boy.

Jake sits up. Woozy. Blinking back to reality. Percy's face comes close to the bars between their cells, taunting:

> ### PERCY (CONT'D)
> My daddy's comin' for me. He learned how
> to kill a man slow from the Apaches. I'm
> gonna watch you suffer a long, long --

Without looking at him or getting up, Jake reaches LIGHTNING QUICK through the bars, grabbing Percy and SLAMMING HIS HEAD INTO THEM, knocking him out COLD.

EXT. CATTLE RANGE - NIGHT

Torchlight illuminates one of the DEAD COW CARCASSES in the now-scorched cattle range. A BOOTED FOOT kicks at it -- TILT UP to the back of a MAN IN SILHOUETTE. Formidable, a mystery. O.S., WHIMPERING SOUNDS bring us to ROY MURPHY, terrified, the drunken cowhand. FIVE MEN (favor two: GREAVEY and JED PARKER) tie his limbs to two HORSE SADDLES:

ROY MURPHY

<u>Please</u>! I didn't kill your cattle, Colonel Dolarhyde, you gotta believe m --

The imposing silhouette LIFTS A FINGER to silence Roy . . . TURNS to us against the torchlight: WOODROW DOLARHYDE. A man accustomed to commanding the land and all its creatures -- now confounded by the cows around him, and an air of being AMUSED by the audacity of the lie he's hearing:

DOLARHYDE

You only been ridin' for my brand, what . . . 'bout 2 weeks. You don't maybe know who you're dealing with, Roy. Nobody calls me "Colonel." Ones that did that are all dead.
> (beat, to let that LAND)

Now: you, Ed, Little Mickey was s'posed to be picking up strays . . . how many you get?

ROY MURPHY

> (terrified)

. . . b-bout 30, Boss . . .

DOLARHYDE

You say you weren't drinkin' . . . I can smell it on you. Don't you respect my rules, Mister? What kinda man blows up other people's cows . . . tells me a bullshit story? Couldn't do no better than that? Where's the other 18 animals, Roy?

ROY MURPHY

It's like I said . . . there were lights
. . .

DOLARHYDE

So there's these big "lights," you fall in
the river, when you come up . . . two of
my oldest hands was just "disappeared."
And there's these exploded . . .
> (voice tails; looks around at
> the cow carcasses)

There wasn't no storm last night, no
lightning. You don't respect me, do you?
Otherwise you wouldn't lie to me . . .
would you?

Dolarhyde draws a BOWIE KNIFE.

DOLARHYDE (CONT'D)

Funny thing about respect. When it's
gone, it's all over, everything gets
sideways . . . I can't have that. Know
what I'm saying, Roy?

Roy's crotch blooms with a PISS STAIN . . . as HOOFBEATS
interrupt: COLORADO and the men are returning from town.
As they REAR, Dolarhyde's eyes narrow:

DOLARHYDE (CONT'D)

Where's Percy?

NAT COLORADO

> (respect + fear)

Taggart locked him up, Boss.

DOLARHYDE

WHY? For WHAT? What the hell'd he do
now?!

NAT COLORADO

Shot a deputy.

DOLARHYDE

. . . God-DAMMIT.

The nervous horses JOSTLE a little at Dolarhyde's ANGER --
STRETCHING Murphy with each small movement:

NAT COLORADO

    He didn't kill him.

DOLARHYDE

    Who's Taggart think he <u>is</u>?! It's <u>my</u> town.
    He wouldn't have a job if I wasn't the
    one keeping that bar open!

 -- Roy's being stretched tight enough to SNAP -- CALLS OUT
IN PAIN, but Dolarhyde ignores it, focused on Nat:

DOLARHYDE (CONT'D)

    Now I gotta go in there, <u>reason</u> with him
    . . . 'cause of <u>your</u> failure to take care
    of my son. Didn't I tell you to watch
    the boy?!

And STABS the knife down . . . SLICING the rope tethered
to Roy's FEET. His lower body SLUMPS to the ground, he
breathes a SIGH:

ROY MURPHY

    <u>Thank</u> y --

Dolarhyde SLAPS the horse's rump, to which Roy's UPPER
TORSO is tied; it GALLOPS off, dragging a SCREAMING ROY
into the night. Dolarhyde closes in on Nat, like he might
hit him. Nat just stares at the ground. Finally, Dolarhyde
moves off --

DOLARHYDE

    <u>Everyone saddle up</u>.

NAT COLORADO

    Boss, we ought to bring some extra hands.

Dolarhyde STOPS. Turns back --

DOLARHYDE

    What for?

NAT COLORADO

> You ain't gonna believe it . . . but I
> think Lonergan's in town.

Dolarhyde's eyes WIDEN -- what?!

DOLARHYDE

Jake Lonergan?

INT. SHERIFF'S OFFICE - BACK ROOM JAIL CELL - CONTINUOUS

CLOSE ON JAKE -- who looks up as a KEY turns in the cell
lock. The door OPENS: Sheriff Taggart, two other deputies,
noses broken, GLARING at him. Taggart sees Percy out cold
. . .

SHERIFF TAGGART

> What happened to him?

JAKE

> Couldn't say.

Charlie and a Deputy unlock Percy's cell and drag him out.
Taggart holds a pair of cuffs, approaches Jake:

SHERIFF TAGGART

> Am I gonna need these?

Jake looks around as the handful of Deputies in the
sheriff's office now train rifles directly at Jake.

JAKE

> No. What're the charges?

Taggart looks down at the WANTED POSTER on his desk.

SHERIFF TAGGART

> Arson, Assault, Mayhem, Hijacking -- says
> you robbed the Bullion Coach last month
> with a gang of outlaws including Pat
> Dolan and Bull McCade, which makes you
> accessory to every law they broke, too.

JAKE

> (almost amused)
> That it?

Murder. Lady outta Cottonwood Grove, next
county over -- name of Alice Wills.

Jake's smirk FALLS. Taggart removes Jake's BLACK STETSON
from a hook on the wall, pulls that PHOTOGRAPH from the
inner brim:

SHERIFF TAGGART (CONT'D)

This her?

Jake just stares at the woman in the picture, CONFUSED.
SHAKEN.

JAKE

You telling me I killed that woman?

SHERIFF TAGGART

You tell me.

Jake reels -- he can't. Taggart slips the pic back in the
brim, tosses the hat to Jake, who catches it with his now-
cuffed hands:

JAKE

Why would I carry a picture of a woman I
murdered?

SHERIFF TAGGART

That's for Judge Bristol in Santa Fe to
sort out.
        (opens the cell)
Now, I'm puttin' you in that coach. I
will treat you with respect, but make no
mistake -- if you try and escape, I <u>will</u>
put a bullet in you.

At gunpoint, Taggart PUSHES Jake out the door --

EXT. ABSOLUTION - MAIN STREET - NIGHT

A PRISON WAGON outside the jail. Taggart leads Jake as
Townspeople watch. The Deputies all have guns on him. THE
DOG starts to follow Jake from behind but one of the

Deputies tsks it away. And suddenly ELLA is beside Jake, kept at bay outside the phalanx of gunmen -- trying to get close, desperate, driven:

                              ELLA
          I'm sorry, but I had no choice -- I
          couldn't let you leave.

                              JAKE
          Well, I'm leaving now.

                              ELLA
          I need you.

                              JAKE
          You got something to say, say it.

                              ELLA
          I need to know where you came from.

                              JAKE
          So do I --

                         SHERIFF TAGGART
          Step aside, Miss.

-- the Deputies edge her back as Jake's loaded into the wagon, where we see Percy slowly coming to in the wagon, already shoved into a seat. As Jake settles in across from him, he SEES MEACHAM through the barred window. A flash of SYMPATHY from the preacher as the dog takes a perch beside Ella. Taggart takes out the cuff key:

                    SHERIFF TAGGART (CONT'D)
          Gimme your wrist.

Jake holds out his hands. Taggart unlocks one wrist, freeing a cuff . . . then takes that cuff and LOCKS IT to Percy's wrist:

                    SHERIFF TAGGART (CONT'D)
          Best way to make a man stay put: chain
          him to his enemy.
                    (NUDGES Percy, who starts to GROAN)
          You lovebirds have a nice trip now.

SLAM: The door CLOSES and LOCKS. Jake SIGHS and tries to sit back, but it's hard tethered to Percy, who blinks back to life and realizes who he's chained to . . .

> PERCY
>
> Aw, shit . . .

OUTSIDE, as Taggart turns from the door, he finds EMMETT there:

> SHERIFF TAGGART
>
> What're you doin'? Get on home, go back to bed.

> EMMETT
>
> Please don't go.

> SHERIFF TAGGART
>
> Have to, Emmett. It's my job.

> EMMETT
>
> I don't like it here. Why can't we just leave this place?

> SHERIFF TAGGART
>
> (beat: the party line)
> Well . . . your pa's gettin' things in order. When he does, he'll send for ya.

> EMMETT
>
> What if he doesn't? Been over a year.

A flicker of something in Taggart -- a lie he's having a hard time keeping up. Forces a smile:

> SHERIFF TAGGART
>
> Don't you worry, he will. And this is where your mama's buried -- you know I can't leave my little girl. Now, what would she say if she knew I let you stay up so late?

> DEPUTY LYLE
>> Taggart!

Eight TORCHES become visible on the outskirts of town.

>> SHERIFF TAGGART
>>> (to Emmett)
>> Get under the porch.

Emmett moves off to safety under the porch. Everyone clears the streets as DOLARHYDE'S MEN ride in fast . . .

ON JAKE -- In the wagon. Watching through narrowed eyes. PERCY leans forward, CHUCKLING -- it's <u>on</u>.

Dolarhyde and Nat, the only ones without torches, trot around the coach, peering inside:

>> PERCY
>> I knew you'd come for me, Daddy!!

>> DOLARHYDE
>> <u>Shut up. I'll deal with you later</u>.
>>> (to Nat, re: Jake)
>> That him?

Nat nods. Dolarhyde looks to Taggart:

>> DOLARHYDE (CONT'D)
>> What's my boy doing chained to that outlaw?

Taggart steels himself against Dolarhyde's formidable presence:

>> SHERIFF TAGGART
>> You know I can't let him go. He shot a deputy.

>> DOLARHYDE
>> We can work that out, John. But I want that other fella.
>>> (straight at Jake)
>> <u>Where's my goddamn gold</u>?

ON JAKE -- No clue what he's talking about:

> **JAKE**
> . . . who the hell're you?

> **DOLARHYDE**
> Who the hell am I? Woodrow Dolarhyde.
> I'm the man whose gold you stole off
> the bullion coach two months ago. Year's
> worth of my hard work. Five thousand
> double eagles. I want it back.

Jake's gears are turning, calculating a way out. He BLUFFS:

> **JAKE**
> Why don't you get me outta here . . . we
> can talk about it!

> **SHERIFF TAGGART**
> All right, that's enough.
> > (to Dolarhyde)
> You can handle it with Judge Bristol. I'm
> gonna escort Percy myself, make sure he's
> treated fair.

> **DOLARHYDE**
> I ain't talkin' about him -- Lonergan
> ain't worth nothing to me hangin' from a
> rope. So either you give him to me now.
> Or I'll take him.

> **PERCY**
> What about me?

> **DOLARHYDE**
> I said shut up, boy.

This is gonna get explosive. Taggart's hand hovers over
his holster. The Deputies and Dolarhyde's men follow suit.

> **SHERIFF TAGGART**
> Turn your men around and go home, Woodrow.
> You're not an outlaw.

                              DOLARHYDE
               No, I am not . . . but I _am_ a man who'll
               protect what's his.

          And then . . . the strangest thing. From the other end of
          town, WAAAAY off in the distance, we see . . .

          LIGHTS -- they echo the lights that heralded Dolarhyde's
          arrival, but these are . . . DIFFERENT.

INT. WAGON - NIGHT

          ON JAKE -- IN THE WAGON -- HIS BRACELET

          Starts PULSING RED. The hell? WIND begins to billow. TORCHES
          flicker.

EXT. ABSOLUTION - MAIN STREET - NIGHT

          ANIMALS get SKITTISH. HORSES stamp. The men suddenly have
          to pull the reins to keep them from bolting. DOGS start to
          run out of town.

          OUR DOG stays beside Ella but BARKS. She looks off at the
          incoming lights. Recognition in her eyes. Starts backing
          away:

          THOSE STRANGE LIGHTS

          Coming closer on the horizon, obscured by dust. Moving at
          80 MPH and appear like high-intensity XENON. To 19th-century
          brains, an image that doesn't compute. FEAR spreads --

A NERVOUS DEPUTY glances at Taggart...

OVER TAGGART - In background we see "ANOTHER" GROUP OF RIDERS COMING IN...

CLOSE ON TAGGART as he sees MORE RIDERS COMING IN...

REVERSE as they all look back at the approaching riders. COLORADO: Who the hell are they?

THEIR POV of Riders coming in ....

continuous, SUDDENLY THE LIGHTS ARC SKYWARD...

continuous, EXCEPT ONE LIGHT COMES RIGHT AT THEM...

EVERYONE REACTS...

LOW ANGLE, TILT-UP as FIRST LIGHT passes overhead...

HIGH ANGLE as EVERYONE REACTS...

INT. GOLD LEAF SALOON - CONTINUOUS

A RUMBLING SOUND makes windows SHAKE. DOC and MARIA react
--

INT. WAGON - CONTINUOUS

JAKE'S BRACELET -- the pulsing growing MORE FREQUENT --

The horses are really BUCKING now -- some THRASH MADLY and
men are THROWN from their saddles as the animals STAMPEDE.

EXT. ABSOLUTION - MAIN STREET - NIGHT

AND NOW, THE LIGHTS Mushroom out in THREE DIRECTIONS -- one
SHOOTING UP -- the other two VEERING OFF -- we STAY with
the light traveling upward as it reaches its peak --

EXT. ABSOLUTION - MAIN STREET - NIGHT

ON MEACHAM -- eyes wide as he looks to the brilliant light,
FEAR and AWE:

                          MEACHAM
          Jesus God --

AND THE LIGHT DIVE BOMBS THE TOWN! SOMETHING FIRES DOWN
-- A CABLE -- UNSPOOLING -- A BOLO AT THE END COILS AROUND
A MAN STILL ON HORSEBACK AND RIPS HIM FROM THE SADDLE --
HURTLING HIM, SCREAMING, THROUGH THE AIR AS HE'S PULLED UP
INTO THE LIGHT!!!

Yeah, these are HIGH-TECH LASSOS. PANDEMONIUM. The other two
flying lights roar into the town in a tri-attack formation,
kicking up impossible dust. Visibility falls to near zero.

The lights STREAK THROUGH FRAME. We GLIMPSE what they're
attached to --

SPEEDING ALIEN CRAFTS -- Helpless VICTIMS are YANKED OFF
THE GROUND and PULLED into the light like roped steer.

Men start FIRING at the lights, but the return fire comes
as INCENDIARY PULSE BEAMS THAT SHRED THE TOWN. Buildings
explode like matchsticks. Absolution is suddenly a burning,
smoky hell.

THE PRISON COACH -- Deputy Lyle's thrown from the top as it careens down the road, then SLAMS into debris -- UPENDING -- FLIPPING SIDEWAYS as the horses try to break free --

INT. PRISON WAGON - CONTINUOUS

Jake and Percy TUMBLE end over end -- SLAMMING into walls, LOCKED TOGETHER --

EXT. ABSOLUTION - MAIN STREET - CONTINUOUS

DOC AND MARIA -- SEPARATED in the melee -- he sees her across the street and RUNS for her -- but **WHAM!** A BOLO CLAMPS MARIA AND YANKS HER BACKWARD, SCREAMING! Doc LEAPS after her but she's GONE --

                              DOC
        MARIA!!!

INT. PRISON WAGON - CONTINUOUS

JAKE AND PERCY -- TRAPPED IN THE UPSIDE-DOWN COACH -- suddenly, JAKE'S BRACELET ACTIVATES! METAL COMING TO LIFE, coiling up around his arm -- WHAT? HOW? -- as it becomes . . .

A BLASTER WEAPON!

                         PERCY
        How you do that?!

BLLLL-AMMM! IT FIRES A PULSE, SMASHING THROUGH THE SIDE OF THE COACH. THE RECOIL HURTLES JAKE AND PERCY BACK. Regaining his balance:

                          JAKE
        STOP PULLING AND GIMME YOUR HAND! --

           PERCY   JAKE
   -- THE HELL FOR?! --   -- I CAN GET US FREE!
                                 GIMME YOUR DAMN HAND!!!

Percy RELENTS. Offers up his hand. Jake grabs all of Percy's FINGERS -- CRRRRAAACK! HE SNAPS THEM BACKWARD!

Percy SHRIEKS as Jake KICKS him back against the wall, FORCING Percy's hand out of the cuff -- now Jake's UNTETHERED, too! He LEAPS OUT of the gaping hole . . .

EXT. ABSOLUTION - MAIN STREET - CONTINUOUS

ON DOLARHYDE -- As he sees PERCY tumble from the coach a beat later --

                          PERCY
          MY FINGERS!! HE BROKE MY FINGERS!!!

As Dolarhyde races toward his son . . . **KLINK**! A bolo CLAMPS around Percy's neck and he's YANKED OFF, TOO! Dolarhyde SEES HIS SON DISAPPEAR UP INTO A PASSING LIGHT:

EXT. ABSOLUTION - MAIN STREET - CONTINUOUS

Taggart pushes through bodies and chaos, sees building deck boards stripped away like piano keys, EXPOSING EMMETT HIDING BENEATH THEM. Taggart runs, pulling him from the wreckage --

                     SHERIFF TAGGART
          EMMETT!

                          EMMETT
          What's happening?!

                     SHERIFF TAGGART
          Stay by my side! You're gonna be oka --

A BOLO CLAMPS AROUND THE SHERIFF, SNAPS TAUT, and RIPS HIM OUT OF HIS GRANDSON'S HANDS! Emmett SCREAMS as ANOTHER BOLO lashes toward the boy, but at the last second ELLA tackles him aside --

                          EMMETT
          THEY TOOK HIM! LEMME GO!!!!

But she just GRABS Emmett and pulls him into an ALLEYWAY, CLINGS HIM to her to keep him safe. He STRUGGLES but she's TOO STRONG:

EXT. ABSOLUTION - MAIN STREET - CONTINUOUS

ON JAKE -- As one of the flying lights circles toward him -- BLASTING LASER FIRE at shooting Cowboys --

Everyone runs in the other direction, but Jake moves toward an approaching light, another craft swooping in -- he raises his arm, aiming, holding his ground and reflexively, his WRIST WEAPON FIRES ANOTHER BLAST -- KABOOM! The incredible firepower HITS!

The craft SPIRALS OUT OF CONTROL -- ROARS inches over Jake's head -- CRASHES onto the main drag, PLOWING through muddy ground, kicking up a trail of FIRE and DEBRIS.

The other lights VANISH back into the sky . . . GONE.

Then, SILENCE. Jake stares at the bracelet, speechless.

EMMETT and ELLA emerge from the alley. All in shock.

And for the longest beat . . . nobody seems to remember how to speak. As they all look . . . to JAKE.

ON DOLARHYDE -- Staring at Jake like he might be a cobra ready to strike. Ventures a step forward, tentatively . . .

                    DOLARHYDE
          What -- are those things?

                    JAKE
          Why're you asking me?

Dolarhyde takes another careful step, pointing at Jake's BRACELET . . .

                    DOLARHYDE
          You shot it -- with that iron. Where'd
          you get it? It was shooting the same
          kinda lights they were.

DOC stumbles up, dazed, mind tumbling . . .

                                   DOC

          What the . . . hell was that? They got . . .
          Maria . . . they took my wife . . .

                                  EMMETT
                                 (crying)
              . . . they got my Grandpa . . .

A PSSSSSSSSS cuts them off. Coming from the CRASHED SPEEDER
down the main drag. Jake WHIRLS -- blaster READY. Dolarhyde's
pistol snaps up. too. Two gunfighters side by side -- the
tension between them THERE but ON HOLD for now as:

Slowly . . . they start walking toward the craft.
Dolarhyde's eyes flick to that blaster on Jake's wrist,
back to the crashed ship in the distance. Ass end in the
air, nose cone BURIED.

Jake and Dolarhyde reach it. The others wait behind, Doc
calls out:

                                   DOC

          You see anyone in there? Is -- my is wife
          in there?!
                           (no response)
          HEY!

                               DOLARHYDE

          No, she's not here!!
                        (long beat; then, re: the craft)
          Is it dead?

Jake kicks it lightly with his boot . . .

                                   DOC

          It's metal.

                                  EMMETT

          Is it demons?

He looks right to Meacham. The preacher stammers, caught
off guard . . .

                    MEACHAM
        I don't right know what it is . . . but
        it sure fits the description.

That sits in SILENCE.

                      DOC
        Well, what the hell does that mean? Jesus
        Christ, Preacher, what the hell does that
        mean, "demons"? Bible stuff? Talkin' bout
        the Good Book? Hellfire and all that?

                    MEACHAM
        Calm down, Doc . . . you're scarin' the
        boy.

                      DOC
        Calm down? You telling me a bunch of
        demons came and took my wife -- took our
        people -- and you want me to calm down?!

SUDDENLY -- behind Doc, something BLURS PAST, on, the,
ROOFTOPS -- THUMP THUMP THUMP -- a SHAPE -- moving from
roof to roof -- then GONE -- people FREAK, draw weapons,
trying to FOLLOW the sounds:

                    TOWNSFOLK
        WHAT IS IT?! WHERE'D IT GO?!! THERE! NO,
        THERE!!!

SMASH! Whatever it is, it just CRASHED through the side
of a BUILDING -- wood flies -- from within, we hear women
SCREAMING in terror -- then BANG BANG! Through a dark
window, SHOTGUN MUZZLE FLASHES -- then a MAN'S SCREAM
as his gun's ripped away, followed by HORRIFIC SOUNDS --
MONSTER SOUNDS --

THE WINDOW -- as SPLAT: the shooter's INSIDES SPRAY the
glass!

Everyone REACTS, then SMASH! The unseen thing CRASHES out the
other side of the building, landing in an alley BEHIND IT.

ANGLE - THROUGH SLATTED FENCE

We see a TALL SHAPE MOVING FAST, racing away from town.
Everyone rushes over to see, in the FAR DISTANCE:

Some kind of CREATURE is skittering into the night. GONE.

Now, people are trying to control the near hysteria they
all feel. A long, impossible silence. Lyle shakes from the
trance, sees the terrified boy staring into the night --

                    DEPUTY LYLE
        C'mon, let's get you back inside --

He leads Emmett toward the Sheriff's office --

JAKE'S BLASTER -- suddenly retracts, folding in on itself.
A BRACELET once again. He's as confused as everyone else --

                    DOLARHYDE
        How'd you do that?

Jake just stares --

                        JAKE
        I got no idea.

                    DOLARHYDE
        Do it again.

                        JAKE
            (dumbfounded)
        I can't.

                    DOLARHYDE
        Where the hell did you get it?

                        JAKE
        For the last goddamn time: I. Don't.
        Remember.

                    DOLARHYDE
        What do you mean, "You don't remember?"

                              NAT COLORADO (O.S.)
                   I found tracks!

EXT. ABSOLUTION STREET - NIGHT

Nat's kneeling by the imprint of a TALONED ALIEN FOOT. Doc
and Jake there, too. They see the tracks head out of town.
Dolarhyde now holds a SHOTGUN. Everyone stares, shocked,
terrified . . .

                              DOC
                  . . . what the hell is that?

                         NAT COLORADO
                  Not like any tracks I've ever seen.

                          DOLARHYDE
                  Whatever the hell they are, they're
                  headed west with our kin.
                         (to his men)
                  Find the horses. We're going after it
                  before we lose the trail.

The men trade reluctant looks --

                       DOLARHYDE (CONT'D)

I said move!

And they do --

                              DOC
                  Wait a minute, what do you mean you're
                  going after 'em? What're you going after,
                  pal? What the hell you planning to do?

Jake turns abruptly, starts heading off --

                          DOLARHYDE
                  Hey.

Dolarhyde moves toward him --

DOLARHYDE (CONT'D)

Didn't you hear what I said?

JAKE

I heard what you said. I don't work for
you.

DOC

Did you hear what I said? What exactly
you got in mind?!

DOLARHYDE
(ignoring Doc; re: the bracelet)
I need that thing. It's the only weapon
that counts. And you owe me.

JAKE

I don't see it that way.

In a flash, Dolarhyde CRACKS THE BUTT OF HIS SHOTGUN INTO
JAKE'S JAW! The only man who shares Jake's gunfighter speed.

Jake absorbs the strike, PUNCHES BACK, sending Dolarhyde's
shotgun flying out his hand. Nat's about to jump in, but
Dolarhyde freezes his gang with a gesture.

Everything stops. Everyone stares. Jake backs away, hand on
his gun, not taking his eyes off Dolarhyde:

DOLARHYDE
(finally, low)
. . . Let him go . . .

Jake moves off. Around a corner. GONE.

ON ELLA -- Troubled, desperate for him not to leave.

ON DOLARHYDE. Grim. Hateful eyes. To Nat:

DOLARHYDE (CONT'D)

Start packin' the horses. We leave at
dawn.

BEGIN INTERCUT SEQUENCE:

EXT. DESERT PLAINS - DAWN

Jake RIDES HARD. Running from his demons, or maybe toward them.

                    MEACHAM (V.O.)
          Recall the Book of Numbers: God commanded
          Moses into the promised land of Canaan
          . . .

EXT. ABSOLUTION - MAIN STREET - SUNRISE

Emmett helps a LITTLE GIRL pull her half-burnt DOLL from the rubble . . .

                    MEACHAM (V.O.)
          But Moses sent his spies to survey the
          land, and they returned with fearful
          hearts . . . for they'd seen giants
          there, evil beings more powerful than
          they'd ever encountered. "We can't
          survive against them," they said. And for
          their fear, they were forced to live in
          exile for the rest of their days . . .

Amidst debris, Meacham finds his BIBLE on the ground. Determination in his eyes, he picks it up --

EXT. PLAINS OUTSIDE ABSOLUTION - DAY

Jake stops on a ridge, sensing a presence behind him: a RIDER in the valley below. Someone's FOLLOWING him. His eyes narrow --

As we go BELOW, to reveal the rider's identity: ELLA. Seeing him disappear over the ridge. SPURS her horse onward . . .

INT. GOLD LEAF SALOON - DAWN

Triage area. Doc moving through with others, tending to the WOUNDED. Amid the carnage, all the pain and wracked faces, he looks up at the RISING SUN out the window. Suddenly,

grimly, infused with PURPOSE . . . over this, Meacham's
WORDS:

> ### MEACHAM (V.O.)
> . . . but the few that had faith in
> God's grace stood tall against the
> giants, and they were allowed to enter
> into the promised land . . .

EXT. ABSOLUTION - MAIN STREET - DAY

AND NOW WE CATCH UP TO WHERE MEACHAM'S VOICE IS COMING
FROM:

He's standing amid the rubble, his words a sermon/call to
arms --

> ### MEACHAM
> If those creatures are proof of hell,
> then they're also proof of God. He's
> testing our faith -- so we're goin' after
> our kin. Thy will be done, Lord, and
> there's an amen behind it.

EXT. ARROYO - NEAR TREE - DAY

Ella rides up to the ridge where Jake was, to find . . .
Jake's HORSE. But NO JAKE. As she realizes what she's
walked into:

WHAM -- Jake's hand -- out of nowhere -- GRABS ELLA from
behind and YANKS HER OFF THE SADDLE -- SLAMMING her to the
ground, STRADDLING her -- PINNING her arms to the ground
fiercely:

> ### JAKE
> You come clean right now or I swear I'll
> kill you.

> ### ELLA
> They took my people, too.

Her PAIN cuts through his anger, her eyes alive with memory.

ELLA (CONT'D)

I've been looking for them a long time. I
know you can help me find them.

Every instinct in Jake says <u>NO</u> -- because the more he feels
for her, the more he wants to run. Lets her go:

JAKE

Stop following me.

Quickly hops back on his horse. She rises, pleading:

ELLA

<u>I can help you</u>.

But he rides away . . . LOSS in her eyes . . .

EXT. ABSOLUTION - MAIN STREET - DAY

Rifles are COCKED. Dolarhyde and Colorado mount up. Now he
notices Doc climbing onto a saddle . . .

DOLARHYDE

Where the hell you think you're going?

DOC

I'm coming with you.

DOLARHYDE

You're dead weight.

Doc holds Dolarhyde's look -- TOUGH and DETERMINED:

DOC

I'm dead weight? I'm a <u>doctor</u>. You <u>need</u>
me. They took my wife, you hear me? I
stand just as much a chance as any one of
you. You don't like that? Tough.

Stare-off. Finally, Dolarhyde heels past Doc, Colorado
following:

DOLARHYDE

Suit yourself.

Dolarhyde turns to his REMAINING MEN (6), sees them trade worried glances:

                    DOLARHYDE (CONT'D)
          Somebody got something to say?

A beat, then GREAVEY clears his throat nervously:

                       GREAVEY
          What if . . . they're already dead, Boss?

                      DOLARHYDE
          They were roping people, you understand?
          That was a <u>roundup</u>. If they wanted to
          kill them, they would've.

The other ranch hands look at each other. Greavey finally says to the others -- low, resentfully:

                       GREAVEY
          You heard the Colonel.

They mount up and ride off. As we notice . . .

ELLA returning, having witnessed this. Clocking tone and body language. Nearby, Meacham slings a RIFLE over his shoulder -- she says, respectfully:

                        ELLA
          If it's all the same, I'd like to ride
          along, too.

                       MEACHAM
          Your choice, Miss.

EMMETT approaches, leading a PONY. The DOG comes up to him, wagging its tail loyally. Emmett pets the animal, a SWEET COMFORT to the scared, lonely kid.

                       EMMETT
          Come on, boy . . . you can come with me
          . . . good boy . . .

He looks up at Deputy Lyle and Meacham, who shakes his head:

                              MEACHAM
             Can't come, Son. Too dangerous.

                              EMMETT
             I ain't stayin' with these folks. Besides,
             how do you know it's safer here?
                    (Meacham hesitates)
             Come on, I'll water your horse, do
             whatever you say . . . you're all I got
             now.

And that's the truth.

                          DEPUTY LYLE
             I'll look after him on the ride.

Meacham sighs -- no choice . . . finally:

                              MEACHAM
             Go fill your canteen.

He SLAPS the reins and trots off. Emmett GRINS and mounts
the pony, trotting after the rest of them, and we BOOM
UP to show our people (and dog) riding off. MUSIC CARRIES
THROUGH:

EXT. DESERT PLAINS - DAY

EPIC VISTAS OF THE WEST:

  -- As they cross the stunning desert . . .

  -- The sky grows gray with OMINOUS CLOUDS. We're traveling
DEEPER into the heart of darkness . . .

EXT. PLAINS - DAY

JAKE crests a hill. Slowing his horse. The area seems
somehow FAMILIAR to him.

Up ahead, he sees DEBRIS . . . part of a ROOF, lying broken
on the ground. Pieces of a CHIMNEY. He trots closer, to
REVEAL:

EXT. ABANDONED CABIN - DAY

A DESTROYED LOG CABIN. Walls partially TORN AWAY. Something in Jake is DEEPLY STIRRED. Dismounts, tentatively . . . walks up to the PORCH. Boots CRUNCH over broken window glass as he ENTERS:

INT. ABANDONED CABIN - CONTINUOUS

LIGHT BEAMS stream in. Eerie quiet. Jake takes it in, HAUNTED.

INT. CABIN - DAY

MEMORY FLASHCUT! *FRESH FLOWERS in a woman's hand . . . THE WOMAN FROM JAKE'S PICTURE. As she puts them in a glass vase. Sensing someone behind her, she turns --*

Jake stands in the doorway. She grins, relieved . . . her heart full at the sight of him. And to our great surprise, Jake RETURNS THE SMILE. Clearly happy to see her.

> THE WOMAN
>
> *You're back . . .*

He moves to the table and empties the SADDLEBAG he carries across his shoulder. GOLD COINS spill out.

She looks at the coins . . . her face DARKENS:

INT. ABANDONED CABIN - DAY

BACK TO PRESENT - JAKE: REELING. What is this memory? Who is this woman?

Something GLINTS in the far wall where the chimney used to be:

A GOLD COIN EMBEDDED in the wood. Jake pulls it out of the wall, a thousand questions in his eyes. Sunlight SHIMMERS off it and --

INT. CABIN - DAY

MEMORY FLASHCUT! *The cabin is VIBRATING like a tuning fork -- the gold coins SHAKE and drop on the table -- the flower vase*

Jake returns to cabin   SC 37
                             REAL-TIME

"Cabin Flashbacks" 4.

SC 38, 39
REAL-TIME

crunches
dried dead
flowers

SC 40
Flashback

REVEAL
Alice...

cont'd

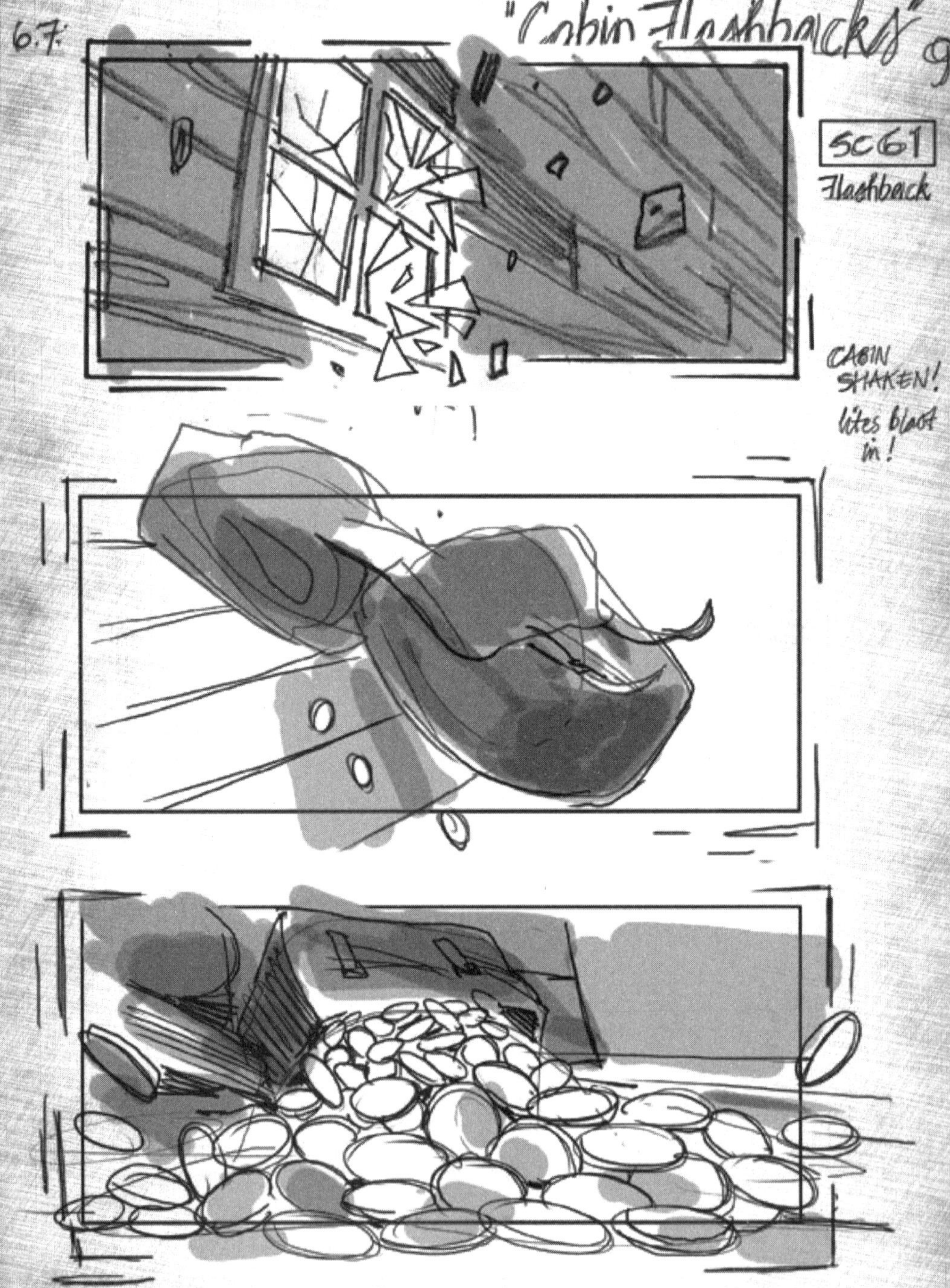

"Cabin Flashbacks" 9

SC 61
Flashback

CABIN
SHAKEN!
lites blast
in!

6.7.10

"Cabin Flashbacks" 13

SC 42

Flashback

gold is
"ferro-
fluided"
up & out

contd

WHIP
TILT

tumbles and SHATTERS -- Jake and The Woman look terrified --

THE WOMAN
What's happening?!!!

JAKE -- pulling her back, panic -- as the coins start distorting in some WEIRD EFFECT; in fact, insanely, they seem to be melting . . .

WINDOWS EXPLODE! <u>THE ROOF'S RIPPED AWAY!</u> The Woman SCREAMS --

KA-CHINNNG! A STEEL BOLO SHOOTS DOWN FROM THE LIGHT, PULLING HER UP INTO IT -- JAKE REACHES FOR HER, BUT IT'S TOO LATE!

INT. ABANDONED CABIN - DAY

BACK TO PRESENT - JAKE

Now he knows. It was THEM. Whoever she was, <u>the creatures took her.</u> Jake stares up at the sky through the hole in the roof . . . with NEW DRIVE.

EXT. DESERT PLAINS - DAY

Our people RIDE. One of Dolarhyde's ranch hands, JED PARKER, travels alongside Doc. Enjoys ribbing him:

JED PARKER
Don't even know why we're going. You know they're all dead.

Doc keeps his eyes forward. Knows he's being toyed with and does his damnedest not to let it rattle him: a "fuck you" smile:

DOC
If they wanted to kill 'em, they would've.

PARKER
Well, if the Boss is right and they <u>was</u> ropin' 'em . . . bet it's to <u>eat</u> 'em. If it was me? I'd start with your wife.

Now Doc looks right at Parker -- a "fuck you" grin:

DOC

You gonna be like this the whole trip?
Cause if y'are, we aren't gonna have a
lotta long conversations. Why don't you
sing a song of something, make yourself
useful . . .

Parker SNEERS and heels onward. Meacham looks over at Doc,
knows he's trying not to look and feel emasculated . . .

MEACHAM

Give you a little friendly advice?
    (Doc glances over)
Get yourself a gun and learn how to
shoot.

WITH ELLA -- As GREAVEY (the other ranch hand) trots up
beside her. He grins, cocky swagger:

GREAVEY

So . . . what's a pretty lady like y --

ELLA

I'm not here to breed.

Beat. Cut down a peg, Greavey tips his hat:

GREAVEY

Well oh-kay.

And rides on. Dolarhyde, having witnessed this, trots up
to her . . . looks at her, tough:

DOLARHYDE

What're you doing here? Woman wandering
alone through Apache country . . . nobody
'round seems to know who you are.

She looks at him. Very directly:

ELLA

The men call you "Colonel" behind your
back, but they're afraid to do it in
front of you. Why?

That lays him bare so unexpectedly -- she's violating defensive boundaries NOBODY violates.

> DOLARHYDE
> All right, you don't wanna tell me?
> That's your business.

She just holds her stare. Unblinking. Then . . . SEES SOMEONE coming over the dunes . . . JAKE. Dolarhyde sees him too:

> DOLARHYDE (CONT'D)
> Well, look who grew a pair.

Jake rides up. Eyes hard. Dolarhyde trots over, the men stare -- off on horseback. Dolarhyde chuckles:

> DOLARHYDE (CONT'D)
> I see you. But I don't see my gold.

> JAKE
> What say we find those people first
> . . . then you can take your best shot
> at collecting.

Dolarhyde smirks, lethal:

> DOLARHYDE
> Right now, the reward on your head might
> be a more promising proposition. Or I can
> put a bullet in your chest and cut that
> bracelet off your wrist.

Jake smirks back, equally killer:

> JAKE
> You know where to find me.

> DOC
> Can't we just be happy the guy with the
> big gun's back?

Jake and Dolarhyde HOLD the look. Tense. Finally, Jake rides on; Doc, Emmett, Ella, and Meacham follow, Dolarhyde and his men trailing behind. The Preacher grins to Jake, tips his hat:

Welcome back.

                    JAKE
              (a dry beat)
      Lord works in mysterious ways.

Small moment of connection. They heel their horses, but
Ella remains -- grinning lightly at Jake:

                    ELLA
      Much obliged to you, Mr. Lonergan.

Jake nods politely:

                    JAKE
      Well, I ain't done nothin' yet.

Still, she smiles kindly:

                    ELLA
      I appreciate it, all the same.

And we hold on them, as they ride quietly, side by side,
in the setting sun.

EXT. DESERT PLAIN - DUSK

HEAVY RAIN. Our people getting drenched as they ride.
Colorado tracking the ground ahead . . .

                 NAT COLORADO
      Rain's getting too heavy. Gonna wash the
      tracks away.

Dolarhyde looks grim as Jake guides his horse to a bluff.
Puts a hand up for the others to stop -- REACTING to
something. As they all join him, one by one, they react in
SHOCK . . . BOOM UP over them to reveal a SURREAL SIGHT in
the valley below:

A RIVERBOAT. Nose buried, paddlewheels facing the sky, as
if it'd been dropped from the clouds. Long, long beat.
Then --

EXT DESERT PLAIN–HEAVY RAIN, TRACK with our riders as they make their way along the canyon rim...

continuous, WITH RIDERS, TILT-DOWN to REVEAL TWISTED AND BUCKLED WOOD in the foreground...

continuous, as THE GROUP STOPS...

REVERSE as the group SLOWLY WORKS ITS WAY DOWN THE SLOPE—BOOM-UP TO
REVEAL...

continuous, BOOM-UP, TILT-DOWN with riders as they descend.
REVEAL RIVERBOAT BELOW...

PAN with our riders as they approach boat...

INT. RIVERBOAT as our group enters...

                              DOC

          Don't know much about boats, but I'd say
          that ship's upside down.

                          DOLARHYDE

          And it's five hundred miles from the
          nearest river that can hold it.
                    (beat)
          C'mon, let's get out of the rain.

                              DOC

          I ain't goin' anywhere near it.

                          DOLARHYDE

          Suit yourself. Sleep in the rain.

Lyle nods. Dolarhyde starts down into the valley. His men
trade uncertain looks, then follow. As do the others . . .

INT. UPENDED RIVERBOAT - NIGHT

A RATTLESNAKE is coiled around a CHANDELIER . . . except
the chandelier is on the floor and the floor is the CEILING.
Upended gambling tables. WOOD RATS scurry over FOOD. Every
window's SMASHED . . . as if something just TOOK everyone.

ANGLES -- our people have settled in throughout the ship,
at a distance from each other. Tense quiet.

  -- JAKE, moving through the creepy corridors.

  -- ELLA, following him at a discreet distance.

  -- DOC, practicing his holster quick-draw. He fumbles the
pistol, not fast enough. Tries again. Bumbles it. Tries to
twirl the gun in his hand but DROPS it on his foot. MEACHAM
appears behind him. Grins. Holding his RIFLE:

                          MEACHAM
          Occurred to me -- you might do better
          with two hands . . .

-- And finally DOLARHYDE, sitting by a small FIRE made from furniture parts. Colorado across from him, saying nothing. Dolarhyde just stares into the fire. Slices an apple with his Bowie knife. Sees Emmett in the corner, admiring his knife.

> ### DOLARHYDE
> You lookin' at this knife? You like this knife?

Emmett nods. He's the only one without a weapon. Dolarhyde rises, moves to the kid -- SPINS the knife in his hand -- and THROWS it. It EMBEDS in the floor by Emmett, who JUMPS. Dolarhyde glares at the kid, hard as nails:

> ### DOLARHYDE (CONT'D)
> Don't lose it.

Emmett takes the knife and moves off. Dolarhyde returns to his perch by the fire. Looks at Colorado, intuiting something in his expression:

> ### DOLARHYDE (CONT'D)
> You fixin' to say something?

> ### NAT COLORADO
> (a beat)
> I dunno, Boss. What do you think? Is there enough of us here?

> ### DOLARHYDE
> (quietly)
> What else am I gonna do?

> ### NAT COLORADO
> Maybe we should . . . notify the army. Get the cavalry involved.

Dolarhyde looks at Colorado -- low, ANGRY:

> ### DOLARHYDE
> We're not turning this over to some West Pointer, wait for 'em to get on the telegraph and ask Washington which hand

to wipe with. I waited around for 'em at
Antietam to tell me what to do.
>   (beat)
Lost four hundred and twenty-eight men.
Over a goddamn cornfield.

Tense beat. Nothing is said. Until finally, Colorado
ventures, quietly . . .

                    NAT COLORADO
>   Might sound foolish . . . but I used to
>   dream about ridin' next to you in the
>   war.
>   (beat)
>   When you used to tell those stories.

Dolarhyde looks at him. Brow furrowed:

                    DOLARHYDE
>   I don't remember telling you those
>   stories.

                    NAT COLORADO
>   I'd listen when you'd tell 'em to Percy.

Dolarhyde understands the impact of that -- and for a
FLICKER, we see some emotion in his eyes.

                    DOLARHYDE
>   There was nothing I ever did worth
>   dreaming about.

                    NAT COLORADO
>   All the same . . . I liked the stories.

Dolarhyde turns back to the fire. Uncomfortable with the
emotional undercurrent here . . .

                    DOLARHYDE
>   They weren't for you, they were for my
>   son.
>   (beat)
>   Wish he'd listened. Now go check on the
>   horses.

Colorado's on his feet, leaves. Dolarhyde turns back to the fire. A GUNSHOT takes us back to:

INT. RIVERBOAT - CONTINUOUS

Doc and Meacham, now mid rifle lesson. Doc's trying to hit a BOTTLE on a table, but having no luck.

> MEACHAM
>
> Treat her like a woman. Talk to her like one: "You look beautiful, darlin', you're the most beautiful gun I ever seen."

As Doc lines up another shot . . .

> MEACHAM (CONT'D)
>
> Align your sights now. If you're outside, read the wind. Don't pull the trigger, you squeeze it . . . gently.

. . . **BANG!** Doc MISSES the bottle again --

> DOC
>
> Dammit.

> MEACHAM
>
> Keep your hands steady. You can do it.

Doc cracks open the barrel and empties shells, reloads; angry, frustrated . . .

> DOC
>
> Maria was right. I ain't no gunfighter . . . ain't no saloon owner . . .
> (beat)
> That woman's the only one who ever believed in me. All I wanted was to put her in some silk, y'know? Give her a little buttermilk. Show her I could provide a better life.
> (beat)
> It's my fault she got took. If I hadn't brought her to that damn town . . .

Doc's on the verge. Holding it together. Finally . . .

                    MEACHAM
          You're gonna get her back. Y'hear? You're
          settin' things right.

                      DOC
          So you . . . think she's still alive?

And Meacham grins. Hopeful:

                    MEACHAM
          Wouldn't be here if I didn't have faith.

INT. RIVERBOAT - CAPTAIN'S QUARTERS - NIGHT

RAIN WATER pours down from a hole in the ceiling. Drift
to . . .

Jake entering the upside-down engine room with the dog.
Removes his hat -- the PHOTO of the WOMAN in the inner
brim. Stares. Suddenly, pain -- he looks down to see BLOOD
seeping through his shirt. His wound's reopened. Pulls off
the shirt and moves under the water, cleaning the gash. A
beat, he looks up . . .

ELLA is in the doorway. Just staring at him. Unblinking.
Jake steps out from under the water . . .

                     JAKE
          You been standing there long?

                     ELLA
          Yes.
               (beat)

                     JAKE
          Something you need?

                     ELLA
          They did that to you . . .

She comes closer to him to inspect his wound. Something
raw in her face. Something vulnerable. He lets her touch
it . . .

                    ELLA (CONT'D)
          Whoever stitched you didn't do a very
          good job.

She grabs a fallen booze bottle, a cloth napkin. Pours
alcohol on it . . .

                    ELLA (CONT'D)
          Who's the woman in your photograph?

                    JAKE
               (a beat)
          All I know is . . . she got taken when
          I did.

                    ELLA
          So you're going to save her . . .

                    JAKE
          She's the only one who knows who I am.

She kneels, dabbing at the wound, dress-cleaning it.

                    ELLA
          You know who you are . . . you just have
          to remember.

He looks at her. Conflict in his eyes.

                    JAKE
          . . . I can't . . .

                    ELLA
               (softly, encouraging)
          Yes you can.

Their faces so close. As she finishes tying the bandage, he
stops her . . . gently but firmly grips her arm:

                    JAKE
          Now you gotta tell me something.
               (beat)
          Who did you lose?

PAIN in her eyes . . .

                                ELLA
          Everyone who mattered to me.

Their look HOLDS . . . then the dog starts to GROWL. Perks
its head. Then BOLTS off as --

JAKE'S BRACELET STARTS TO PULSE -- Jake and Ella LOCK EYES:

                           ELLA (CONT'D)
          Something's here.

INT. BALLROOM UPPER GALLERY & SPIRAL STAIRCASE - CONTINUOUS

Emmett walks through the ship carrying Dolarhyde's knife --
his new prize. Behind him, broken SHIP EQUIPMENT. Jutting
pieces of metal, gleaming BLACK as moonlight cuts in
through slats.

And JESUS -- one of the metal pieces starts to MOVE behind
the kid -- UNFOLDING LIKE A PILL BUG -- THE ALIEN HAS
BLENDED INTO THE MACHINERY -- ITS BODY RISES TO HEIGHT AT
A FULL 7 FEET . . .

Emmett doesn't see it as he moves on . . .

INT. STATEROOM - CONTINUOUS

Greavey, Jed Parker, and the rest of Dolarhyde's men
HUDDLE, whispering:

                          GREAVEY
               What the hell're we doin' here? We should
               be ridin' in the opposite direction of
               those things --

                          JED PARKER
               We do that, the old man's likely to shoot
               us himself. Only way outta this is --

And suddenly -- RATS! A whole lot of them, scurrying
underfoot -- RACING AWAY FROM SOMETHING. The men startle
and juke around --

LIGHTNING FLASHES, illuminating THE FOOT OF THE ALIEN, behind them!!! In IMPRESSIONISTIC FLASHES, it STRIKES -- crazy fast -- blood SPRAYS -- MEN SCREAM --

INT. CORRIDORS - VARIOUS - CONTINUOUS

REACTIONS THROUGHOUT THE SHIP -- Jake/Ella/Dolarhyde/Doc/ Meacham -- HEARING the screams --

INT. CORRIDOR - NIGHT

Emmett hears it too and RUNS back to the others -- turning corners -- we're MOVING behind him -- HANDHELD -- comes to another staircase and STOPS with a GASP:

TWO EYES under the stairs, shining in the dark. They step forward and . . . it's THE DOG. Emmett SIGHS in relief --

> **EMMETT**
> Dammit, Dog, you scared m --

The dog's lips CURL BACK, teeth bared. GROWLING. Emmett steps back, frightened -- but the dog isn't growling at him:

The kid TURNS, frozen. The CREATURE emerges from darkness behind him. The dog ATTACKS, leaping onto the alien, which BATS it aside -- the dog SKIDS and YELPS -- Emmett SCREAMS, RUNS --

INT. RIVERBOAT - VARIOUS - CONTINUOUS

JAKE AND ELLA -- HEAR the boy's SCREAM -- Jake's bracelet ACTIVATES INTO A WEAPON, he runs --

INT. SPIRAL STAIRCASE TO BALLROOM LOWER GALLERY - CONTINUOUS

EMMETT rushes in -- searching frantically for someplace to hide, as THE ALIEN APPEARS. This is the first time we see it -- though it's still mostly hidden in SILHOUETTE. It doesn't seem to see Emmett, who slowly backs up against the wall . . . knocking loose a FRAMED PICTURE. It SHATTERS on the floor and --

-- before Emmett can GASP, WHAM: THE ALIEN IS LOOMING OVER HIM. THE BOY OPENS HIS MOUTH TO SCREAM BUT NO SOUND COMES OUT AS THE ALIEN ENTERS FRAME, ITS FACE <u>INCHES</u> FROM HIS:

SMALL CLAWS UNFOLD FROM THE CREATURE'S CHEST, SLOWLY POKING AT EMMETT'S CHEEKS, NOSE, MOUTH -- LIKE A BLIND PERSON TOUCHING SOMEONE'S FACE. NARROW SLITS ON ITS FACE BLOSSOM OPEN . . . REVEALING TWO RED EYES.

Emmett is CRYING now. The alien's mouth slowly OPENS, its massive jaw unhinging to reveal ROWS OF RAZOR TEETH . . .

SUDDENLY -- KA-BLAM! The alien's shoulder RIPS OPEN in a gout of ORANGE BLOOD! It SCREECHES and recoils from Emmett --

<u>REVEAL MEACHAM BEHIND THE ALIEN WITH HIS RIFLE</u>:

> **MEACHAM**
>
> GET AWAY FROM HIM!

KA-CHUNK, Meacham re-cocks and FIRES AGAIN -- the alien's HIT twice, SHRIEKS -- as Meacham stops to reload, the alien SPRINGS -- <u>PUNCHING ITS CLAW THROUGH THE PREACHER'S CHEST JUST AS</u>:

JAKE runs into the room to see MEACHAM SKEWERED. He SCREAMS IN RAGE and FIRES LASER BLASTS at the moving alien -- but it SPRINGS away, up the wall, skitters upside down across the ceiling, VANISHING into a hole in the roof. Ella RUSHES to Emmett as Jake RUNS to Meacham, on the floor, dying:

> **JAKE**
>
> Easy, now . . . don't move --
> (TURNS; SHOUTING)
> DOC -- GET IN HERE NOW!

Emmett, held by Ella, screams out through tears:

> **EMMETT**
>
> Meacham!

Meacham's eyes, full of acceptance --

                              MEACHAM

          It's okay, boy . . . I'm going home
          . . .

                               JAKE

          Get him outta here.

Ella pulls Emmett out of the room, not wanting him to
witness Meacham's final moments.

                              MEACHAM
                   (looking back at Jake)
          Get our . . . people back . . .

                               JAKE

          Stop talking. <u>DOC</u>!

But Meacham manages to yank the CROSS CHAIN off his own
neck, forces it into Jake's hand and pulls him close --
EYE TO EYE:

                              MEACHAM

          God don't care who you were, son . . .
          only who you <u>are</u>.

ON JAKE -- AFFECTED. Doc and Dolarhyde rush in -- in shock
-- as Meacham takes his last, bloody gasp. Then dies.

                               DOC

          Oh no . . . Oh, Jesus . . .

He closes his eyes in grief. Even Dolarhyde's affected. Doc
picks up Meacham's rifle, covered in blood . . .

Jake looks down at the cross in his hand, rage filled --

EXT. UPENDED RIVERBOAT/JUNIPER TREES AREA - DAWN

     -- SHLICK: A MAKESHIFT WOODEN CROSS is stabbed into the
ground above a freshly covered GRAVE. Jake steps back,
dirty from digging. Doc, we notice, now has Meacham's rifle
slung over his shoulder. Emmett in the distance, searching,
calling out to --

                              EMMETT

          DOG?!! COME ON, BOY!

Nat's up the ridge, crouched by WET TRACKS in the soggy ground. Dolarhyde, antsy, calls up to him:

> **NAT COLORADO**
> Tracks turn north.

> **DOLARHYDE**
> Where're the rest of the boys?

> **NAT COLORADO**
> (beat; averts his eyes)
> They ran off.

Dolarhyde burns, the sting of abandonment -- starts to mount up.

> **DOLARHYDE**
> Goddamn cowards.

Emmett returns, upset . . .

> **EMMETT**
> Can't find the dog . . .

> **DOLARHYDE**
> Probably dead. Let's go.

> **EMMETT**
> He ain't dead --

Ella puts an arm around the boy, leading him off . . .

> **ELLA**
> It's okay, he'll find us. He'll be fine.

Heartsick, Emmett finally starts to move off with her . . .

> **DOC**
> Wait -- aren't we gonna say something?

> **DOLARHYDE**
> The only one who knew what to say's underground. Isn't it enough we wasted time burying him?

Doc glares, angry and emotional:

                              DOC
              Shame on you. Show some respect.

But Dolarhyde turns and trots off, Nat following. Then,
with regretful looks, Deputy Lyle, Ella, and Emmett too
. . .

Doc turns back to the grave -- staring. Someone steps up
beside him -- JAKE. He looks at Doc: "Go ahead." Glad
to have the company, Doc bows his head, closes his eyes
. . .

                         DOC (CONT'D)
              Uh . . . God protect this man's soul,
              he was a gentle spirit . . . he forgave
              me for not worshipping in your house,
              hopefully you do too.
                    (beat, finding words)
              He spoke of having faith and . . . made
              me feel better. Cut me some slack. World
              was a better place for havin' him.

A sigh, then he looks to Jake, unsure . . .

                         DOC (CONT'D)
              How was that?

Jake nods: "Good enough." Turns to go . . .

                             JAKE
              C'mon.

They head to the horses . . . and we SLAM TO:

EXT. DESERT - APPROACHING BOX CANYON - DAY

TRAVELING SHOTS: Our people RIDING across the desert plains,
advancing at a steady clip as they follow the trail . . .
among these images:

A POV -- FROM THE RIDGE ABOVE: Someone or something is
watching the caravan . . .

COWBOYS
&
ALIENS™

ABOVE: A view of the town of Absolution, featuring Doc's Gold Leaf Saloon at right.

BELOW: Jake prepares to fire on an alien craft during the attack on the town.

LEFT: "Not like any tracks I've ever seen." ABOVE: People converge on the downed craft.
BELOW: The interior of the upside-down riverboat.

ABOVE: Alien ships strafe the rescue party. BELOW: Jake prepares to jump onto the alien vessel.

BELOW: Jake leaps onto the alien craft to rescue Ella.

LEFT: The hypnotic alien light source. ABOVE: The man without a memory (Daniel Craig). BELOW: Jake is surrounded.

LEFT: Jake tests the fit of his new hat. ABOVE: The no-nonsense preacher Meacham (Clancy Brown) is the first person Jake meets in town. BELOW: Doc (Sam Rockwell), the saloonkeeper.

LEFT: Ana de la Reguera is Maria, Doc's wife.
THIS PAGE: Jake arrives in Absolution in search of his past.

ABOVE: Royal Dano is bad boy Percy Dolarhyde. BELOW: A reckless Percy takes up a collection.

ABOVE: Apache half-breed cowhand Nat Colorado (Adam Beach). BELOW: Maria tries to soothe a humiliated Doc.

ABOVE: Sheriff Taggart (Keith Carradine, right). BELOW: The mysterious Ella (Olivia Wilde).

ABOVE: Jake finds himself imprisoned for murder. BELOW: Sheriff Taggart looks ready for trouble.

ABOVE: Deputy Lyle (Brendan Wayne) keeps watch. BELOW: Rancher Woodrow Dolarhyde (Harrison Ford, right). RIGHT: Jake is led to the prison wagon headed for Santa Fe.

ABOVE: Dolarhyde arrives at the sheriff's office in search of Percy but finds Jake, too. BELOW: Doc looks on as Meacham aims his rifle.

ABOVE: Taggart is bewildered by the alien attack. BELOW: Emmett (Noah Ringer) hides under a boardwalk.

ABOVE: Cowboys scatter as aliens stage an attack. BELOW: Dolarhyde fires at the aliens.

ABOVE: Jake faces an alien craft as it sweeps into town. BELOW: Jake and Dolarhyde approach the wreckage.

LEFT: Ella looks for signs of life from the downed speeder.
THIS PAGE: Nat finds tracks he can't identify in the street.

THIS PAGE: Dolarhyde commands the posse that
rides out at dawn after the escaped alien.
RIGHT: Chris Browning is Jed Parker, one of
Dolarhyde's ranch hands.

LEFT: Ella rides with the posse. ABOVE: Nat looks on as Dolarhyde presses his point.
BELOW: Dolarhyde broods at the campfire.

ABOVE: Jake explores the overturned riverboat. BELOW: Jake's weapon lights the way as Ella looks on.
RIGHT: Emmett is heartsick for his abducted grandfather, Sheriff Taggart, and his adopted dog, who goes missing.

ABOVE: Cowboy Roy Murphy (Toby Huss) slacks on the job. BELOW: Walton Goggins is Hunt, an outlaw who recognizes Jake as his boss.

ABOVE: Jake's former associates make trouble. BELOW: Ella and others look on as Jake is roughed up.

ABOVE: Dolarhyde and Doc discuss whether they should step in and help Jake. BELOW: Jake and Ella share a quiet moment.

ABOVE: Jake and Dolarhyde ride out. BELOW: Apache chief Black Knife (Raoul Trujillo) gathers his warriors.

LEFT: Black Knife is suspicious of the white men in his territory. ABOVE: Bronc (Julio Cedillo, left) with Doc. BELOW: Black Knife holds court.

THIS PAGE: Jake takes Apache medicine in the hope that it will unlock memories of the aliens' location.
RIGHT: Seen in a memory, Abigail Spencer is Alice, Jake's true love.

LEFT: Jake and Alice embrace in their cabin by the cottonwood grove. ABOVE: Alice hopes that Jake will reform his outlaw ways. BELOW: Jake remembers that Alice has been abducted by the aliens.

ABOVE: The leaders ride out to meet their destiny. BELOW: Doc proves his courage during the expedition.

ABOVE: Doc comforts the wounded Bronc. BELOW: Emmett keeps watch for the freed captives.

ABOVE: Jake and Ella enter the alien stronghold. BELOW: Jake lights their way with his wrist blaster.

ABOVE: Jake and Ella discover the captives. BELOW: The abductees are in thrall to a glowing light.

ABOVE: Maria is among the hypnotized prisoners. BELOW: Jake and Ella plot their approach.

ABOVE: Jake and Dolarhyde flee the aliens' cavern. BELOW: Jake and others continue to run from the alien freighter. NEXT PAGE: Jake, freed from the past, achieves a bittersweet victory.

JAKE -- riding ahead of the rest, on point. He sees what's on the ridge --

THREE APACHES walking their horses at the same pace and on a course roughly parallel with our group.

Nat takes frame beside Dolarhyde, <u>sotto</u>:

                    NAT COLORADO
          I got him. Tracks are getting closer
          together. He's heading for that canyon.

                    DOLARHYDE
          Good job. I thought we lost him.

Nat now notices:

                    NAT COLORADO
          Apache.

                    DOLARHYDE
          I know. Been back there a while. They
          won't follow us into that canyon. Best
          not to mention it to the others.

Just then, Ella catches up with:

                    ELLA
          I think we're being followed.

                    DOLARHYDE
          We know.

Finally, Jake pulls up next to them:

                    JAKE
          Apaches. Best bet is that canyon.

As they ride on, the Apaches stop. Watching from above.

                    DOLARHYDE
          What the hell do you know?

And he kicks his horse, leading the others ahead.

INT. BOX CANYON - DAY

As they enter a box canyon, Colorado REARS his horse, kneels by another ALIEN FOOTPRINT. Jake and Dolarhyde look around, sensing trouble . . . but nothing visible. Nat looks off --

                          NAT COLORADO
          That way --

BLAMBLAM!!!! GUNSHOTS suddenly PEPPER the ground -- the horses REAR and KICK UP, startled --

A DOZEN FIGURES POP UP ON THE CLIFFS ALL AROUND THEM. Badass OUTLAWS with RIFLES aimed at our heroes. One CALLS DOWN:

                        OUTLAW GUNMAN
          HANDS IN THE AIR!

SHIT. Slowly, everyone's hands go up. Jake raises his hands, unarmed -- as they SEE:

TWO RIDERS -- incoming -- from the other end of the canyon. Rifles aimed and ready. One of the outlaws knocks back the hammer on his rifle --

                          OUTLAW
          I say we just shoot 'em and take their --

But the words catch in his throat as his EYES WIDEN:

                       OUTLAW (CONT'D)
          . . . Boss?

Sure enough, they're looking right at JAKE. Both outlaws (BRONC and HUNT) lower their guns, hostility replaced by SURPRISE:

                           HUNT
          What the hell you doin' back here,
          Lonergan?

Oh, Christ. this is JAKE's gang. ON DOLARHYDE. ELLA. COLORADO. All registering it. And Jake, of course, doesn't REMEMBER these men as Bronc dismounts, nervous:

BRONC

Jesus, Boss . . . Dolan's gonna <u>shit</u> when
he sees you.
              (then; re: the others)
And who the hell're <u>they</u>?

ON JAKE -- How does he handle this? Hunt rides up next
to him, SUSPICIOUS, and for reasons yet to be known,
unfriendly:

HUNT

What's the matter, Jake? Cat got your -- ?

SMACK! Jake SLAPS Hunt across the face, stopping the
question off his tongue --

JAKE

Shut up!

Ella and our people REACT as Jake plays it up, best defense
a good OFFENSE. Dolarhyde looks to Jake: "What the fuck?"
Jake glances back: "Go with it."

The outlaws are scared: <u>This</u> is the Lonergan they know.
Tense beat. Hunt holds his bloody mouth:

HUNT

Christ, Jake . . . you broke my <u>tooth</u>.

JAKE

Then keep your mouth shut.
              (to Bronc)
How many boys we got left?

HUNT

'Bout the same.

JAKE

              (beat)
Still about, uh . . .?

HUNT

30.

                              JAKE
              That's right. 30. Good. Where's my stuff?

Hunt and Bronc trade glances, confused --

                              HUNT
              You took it with you.

                              JAKE
                    (oh)
              Damn right I did. Bring me to the camp.
              Time to set things straight.

Bronc and Hunt nod, mounting up, SHOUTING to the outlaws
above:

                              BRONC
              LONERGAN'S BACK! MEET US AT THE CAMP!

As they RIDE OFF, Dolarhyde looks to Jake and mutters:

                           DOLARHYDE
              This is your gang?

                              JAKE
              So it seems.

Doc leans in, trying to look "tough" as his eyes scan the
other outlaws -- murmurs low:

                              DOC
              Listen, these guys look a bit lonely to
              me. I think it's time to call it a *noche*.

                              JAKE
              We need every gun we can get.

And he SPURS on, leaving the rest of them to follow
uneasily.

EXT. GANG CAMP - DAY

We're in an OUTLAW CAMP: roughly 30 fast guns and saddle
tramps. Tents. Horses. Ample weapons. And right now, most

of them are GEARING UP to ride out for some reason. One of
them, PAT DOLAN, slides a RIFLE into his saddle:

> PAT DOLAN
>
> Flyer's on its way, and we best damn be
> sober for it.

He passes a RED-HAIRED CODGER ("RED") sifting through some
rocks embedded with GOLD NUGGETS. Beside them, WOODEN BOXES
of TNT:

> PAT DOLAN (CONT'D)
>
> How's the haul, RED?

> RED
>
> Gold from the Vulture Mine looks pretty
> rich.

> PAT DOLAN
>
> How much dynamite we get?

> RED
>
> 'Bout fifty sticks.

> HUNT (O.S.)
>
> DOLAN!

Dolan turns; sees HUNT and BRONC crest the hill with the
other OUTLAWS from the cliffs. ANGRILY:

> PAT DOLAN
>
> 'Bout time you got back.
>   (re: Hunt's bloody nose)
> What the hell happened to you?!?

Hunt nods over his shoulder --

> HUNT
>
> He did.

The outlaws part to reveal JAKE, riding in with Ella and
the rest of our people. DOLAN'S eyes NARROW, NOT happy to
see him:

> PAT DOLAN
>
> Well, shit.

It gets very, VERY QUIET. Our people tread warily, knowing whatever reaction Jake's eliciting, it AIN'T GOOD. He runs the gauntlet of ACCUSING GLARES. Smart enough to know that DOLAN is the man in charge. Dismounts:

                         JAKE
          You don't look happy to see me, Dolan.

Dolan eyes him. TOUGH. Clearly, HISTORY here:

                       PAT DOLAN
          You got some balls -- ridin' back here
          like nothin' ever happened.
                    (fuck you)
          No, Lonergan. I ain't happy to see you.

ON JAKE -- How to navigate bad blood that he doesn't REMEMBER?

                         JAKE
          You'll get over it.

Then, pretty much DISMISSING Dolan, Jake turns, addresses the rest of the men. If he's their boss? He's gonna ACT LIKE IT.

                     JAKE (CONT'D)
          Boys? Grab your guns. We're ridin' out.

The men seem . . . CONFUSED. Not sure what the hell is GOING ON.

                         BRONC
          But Jake . . . you -- you said you didn't
          wanna be in charge no more.

And this is a REVELATION. Jake glances at ELLA -- has to keep IMPROVISING to hold his ground:

                         JAKE
          Well, I -- changed my mind. So saddle the
          hell up.

                       PAT DOLAN
          They're not going anywhere with you.
          We're fixin' to rob us a coach.

Uh-oh. Tension. Looks all around. Doc notices a particularly
THUGGY OUTLAW a foot away, staring him down. Just itching
to kill him.

Now Dolan strides forward, right up to Ella. CLOSE. Violates
her space: studies her with a mixture of curiosity and
CONTEMPT.

> ### PAT DOLAN (CONT'D)
> Are you her?

> ### ELLA
> Am I who?

> ### PAT DOLAN
> The whore Jake quit this gang for.

OH. Another piece of the puzzle falls into place -- Jake's
eyes SNAP to Ella as they both REALIZE . . . the men think
she's "Alice." Jake meets Dolan's stare --

> ### JAKE
> Watch your mouth.

> ### PAT DOLAN
> Or what? I run this outfit now.
> (calls out)
> Put your guns on the whore! He so much
> as twitches, blow her brains out her ear.

AT ONCE, 20 GUNS ARE LEVELED AT ELLA'S HEAD. No doubt who
the men are LOYAL to. ON JAKE. OUR HEROES. Shit. But Jake
locks into Dolan, UNFLINCHING:

> ### JAKE
> Call her a whore again, it'll be the last
> word you ever say.

> ### PAT DOLAN
> You ain't in no position to make threats,
> boyo. You're unarmed.

Dolan now turns to BULL MCCADE, roughly the size of a BARN.

                          PAT DOLAN (CONT'D)
              Put him down, Bull.

And Jake barely has time to react as Bull lets fly with a
JAWBREAKING HAYMAKER! Dolarhyde and Nat WINCE as Jake hits
the dirt with a THUD. Dolarhyde murmurs:

                            DOLARHYDE
              Got his hands full here.

                              DOC
              Wanna step in?

                            DOLARHYDE
                       (enjoying this)
              He's doing okay by himself.

Dolan strides up, cock of the walk, LEANS over Jake:

                            PAT DOLAN
              Where the hell's our gold?

Jake SPITS BLOOD, meets eyes with DOLARHYDE, equally alert
at the mention of gold. Jake grins at Dolan, defiant:

                              JAKE
              Don't remember.

Dolan NODS to Bull: SMASH! Another devastating BLOW. ON
ELLA -- At GUNPOINT. Wishing she could intervene. DOC too.

                            PAT DOLAN
              Well, I do remember you tellin' us you
              was leavin' us high and dry because of
              some woman --

 -- WHAM! Bull PUNCHES Jake so hard he FLIES OFF HIS FEET
-- and on the HIT a SOUND FX WHOOSH takes us to:

INT. BEDROOM - NIGHT

MEMORY FLASHCUT! -- *PEACEFUL SILENCE. Jake, shirtless,
stares out a window at the rain. Considering something
huge. Alice comes up behind him, naked, folds her arms
around his chest, presses herself close . . .*

                    ALICE
        It'd be a better life. Clear your
        conscience . . . you don't even sleep a
        full night anymore.

ON JAKE -- Clearly TORN. After a beat of considering,
quietly:

                    JAKE
        It ain't that simple.

                    ALICE
        It is. We can leave all this behind
        . . . make peace with our bad deeds.

                    JAKE
             (a beat)
        Bad's all I was ever good at.

And now. She turns him to her, face to face. Bodies entwined
against the rain-streaked window . . .

                    ALICE
        You're wrong. I know you're a good man
        . . .

As she KISSES him:

EXT. GANG CAMP - DAY

PRESENT: "Good man" ECHOES back to Jake -- he's <u>hit with
the revelation that she was his lover</u>.

ON ELLA -- As we PUSH IN, watching Jake with PURE EMPATHY
--

                    PAT DOLAN
        Guess you just left out the part about
        taking our goddamned gold from that
        coach.

ON DOLARHYDE -- Now he's <u>sure</u> what they're talking about;
to Doc:

                    DOLARHYDE
             (sotto)
        . . . <u>my</u> gold . . .

DOLAN: "BOUT TIME YOU GOT BACK..."

DOLAN:... WHAT THE HELL HAPPENED TO YOU?"

HUNT: "HE DID."

(14)

(15)

(DOLANS P.O.V.)

(16)

10

JAKE: "YOU DON'T
LOOK HAPPY TO SEE
ME, DOLAN."

DOLAN: "YOU GOT
SOME BALLS --
RIDING BACK...?"

> PAT DOLAN
>> (to Jake)
> So I'm gonna ask you one last time --
> where _is_ it?

Dolan PUNCHES Jake again --

EXT. GANG CAMP - DAY

  -- then GRABS Jake's hair and YANKS BACK:

> PAT DOLAN
> I'm gonna ask you one last time . . .
> where's my gold?

Jake looks up, BEATEN -- teeth bloody, focus BLURRING --
his expression is PURE REGRET:

> JAKE
> . . . demons . . .

> PAT DOLAN
> What's that?

> JAKE
> Demons stole your gold . . . when you get
> to hell, you can ask for it back . . .

> PAT DOLAN
>> (tsks)
> That's the way you wanna do it.
>> (turns)
> Kill the whore.

ON THE GANG -- As they all cock their guns -- aimed at Ella
-- this is IT --

Then -- BEEP. BEEP. BEEP. Jake's bracelet starts FLASHING.

A proximity warning. It UNFOLDS! Dolan sees the strange
weapon -- shock -- WHIP-DRAWS his GUN but JAKE'S BLASTER
FIRES! Dolan FLIES BACK 15 FEET, skidding across the dirt.
DEAD.

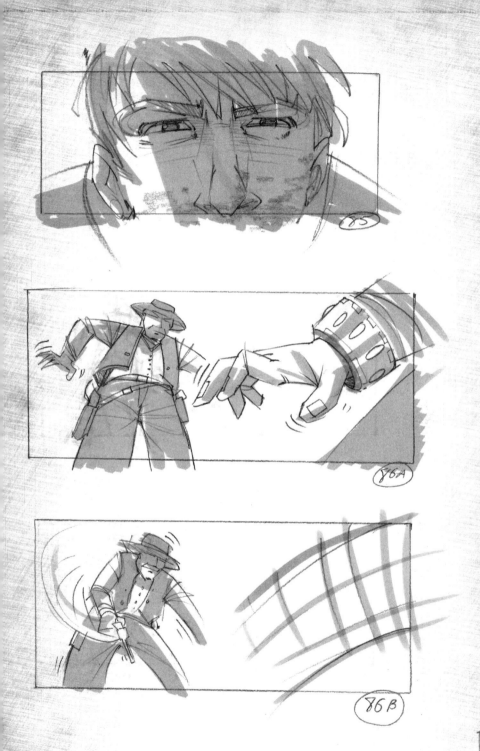

85

86A

86B

39

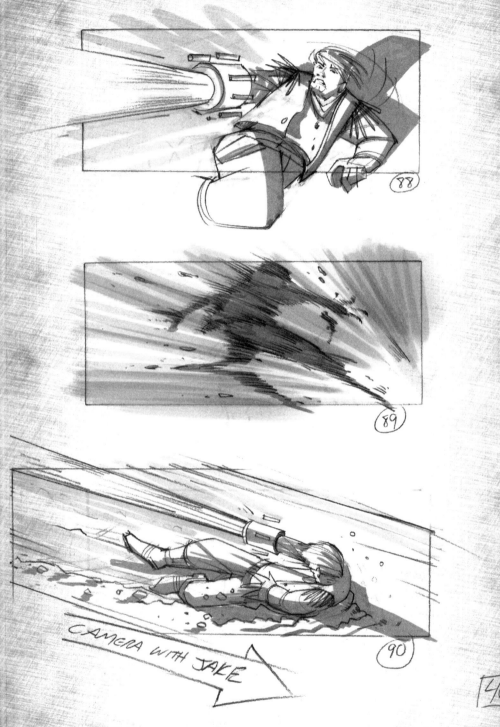

88

89

CAMERA WITH JAKE

90

140

EVERYONE'S FACES. Holy shit.

                         JAKE
              Told you not to call her that.

Jake is pure KILLER. Turns to the speechless Bull McCade
and KICKS HIM IN THE BALLS as hard as he can, doubling him
over.

                      JAKE (CONT'D)
              Everybody drop your guns.

Hunt THROWS his to the ground without pause. Slowly, the
rest comply as Jake backs away, to his team:

                      JAKE (CONT'D)
              Saddle up --

                       DOLARHYDE
               -- what? --

                         JAKE
              On your horses, go -- those things're
              close.

They mount up FAST as Jake holds the gang off with his
blaster. Jake swings onto his own horse --

And they all GALLOP AWAY -- racing into the desert --
leaving the gang behind --

EXT. DESERT PLAINS - MINUTES LATER

Our people RIDE HARD across the open plains -- adrenaline
still PUMPING through them --

Dolarhyde looks over his shoulder, alarmed:

Everyone turns: behind them, JAKE'S GANG. CHASING. Coming
hard in pursuit -- and to make matters worse, Jake's gun
starts BEEPING FASTER. He looks up: on the horizon is a
BILLOWING SAND CLOUD.

YES, FOUR SPEEDERS ARE ROARING IN, ON THE HUNT. AND UNLIKE
THE TOWN ATTACK, THIS TIME WE SEE THEM IN THE HARSH LIGHT
OF DAY:

Quickly, our team WHIRLS their horses around and starts riding in the opposite direction -- no choice -- TOWARD the gang, who FIRES rifles at them -- bullets WHIZ by our people --

But then the gang members SEE THE INCOMING SPEEDERS TOO. STUNNED FACES -- WHAT THE HELL ARE THOSE?! -- now THEY turn tail too and double back where they came from, but it's TOO LATE:

STEEL COLLARS FLY, ATTACHED TO ROPING CABLES -- BEFORE THE GANG KNOWS WHAT'S HAPPENING, THEY'RE BEING GRABBED AND DRAGGED AWAY! THE FIRST TO GO IS DEPUTY LYLE!

Those who have their wits about them FIRE BACK, trying to hit the flying machines. CROSSFIRE. CONFUSION.

Our people spread out -- galloping in separate directions but --

A SPEEDER ROARS IN

Fires two RINGS -- KA-CHANK / KA-CHANK! One grabs JAKE, the other ELLA -- they're RIPPED off horses --

But the collar's grabbed Jake's BLASTER HAND -- DRAGS HIM over desert floor toward the speeder's open maw -- he FIRES his blaster -- SHEARING THE ROPING CABLE and WINGING the speeder --

Line cut, Jake TUMBLES away -- Ella's PULLED UNDER the speeder's wing! Jake staggers up, FIRES again but the ship streaks off --

As a riderless horse gallops past, Jake swoops onto the saddle like a rodeo bulldogger -- HYA! -- GIVING CHASE:

EXT. DESERT PLAINS - NEAR ARROYO - DAY

WHOOSH! The speeder slots into an OPEN CANYON, trailing smoke, flying parallel to a BLUFF -- upon which JAKE appears, riding like hell, trying to keep pace --

WIDE, AERIAL -- Jake's a small figure barreling after the speeder as it DIPS lower into the canyon -- he's gonna lose it:

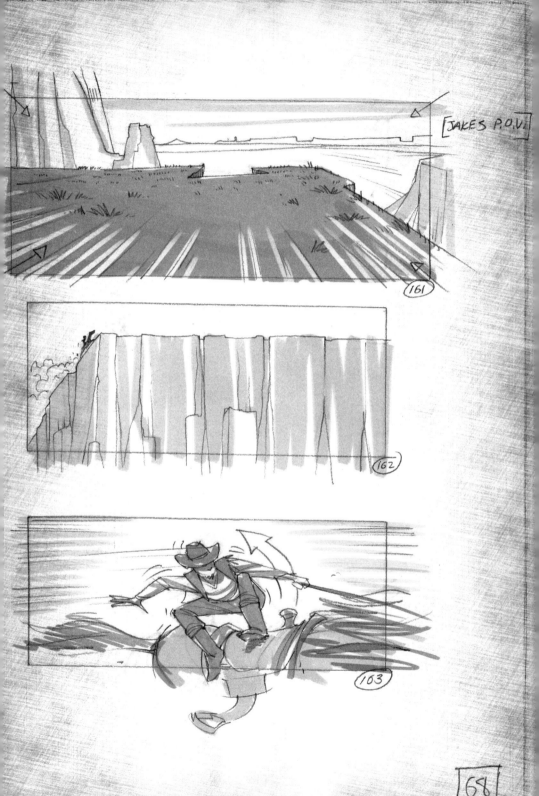

JAKES P.O.V.

161

162

163

68

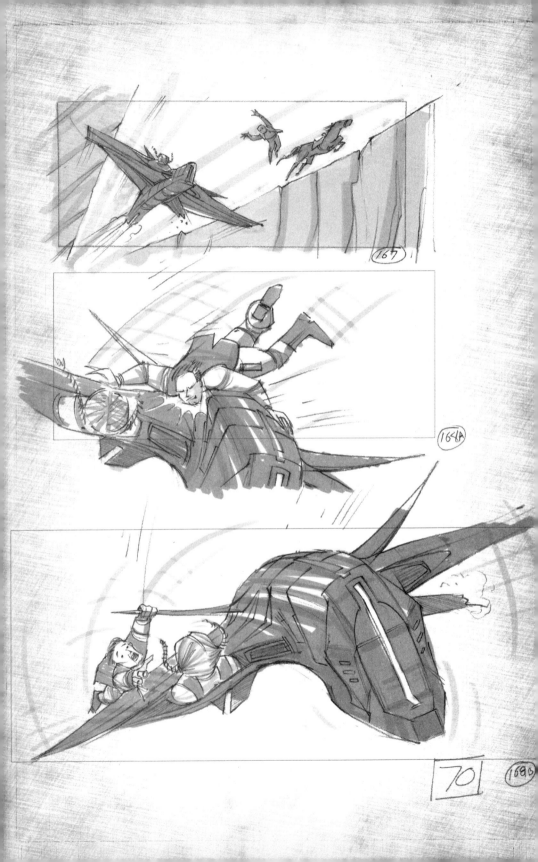

And Jake makes a CHOICE: SWINGS himself side-saddle, and ONE, TWO . . . THREE: JUMPS, LEAPING OUT INTO OPEN SPACE!

LANDING HARD, PAINFULLY, AND ONLY BARELY, ON THE CRAFT'S WING -- manages to get a grip and HANG ON as the already-damaged ship SHUDDERS and DROPS from the unexpected weight --

Now it's SKIMMING low to the ground at 80 MPH -- low enough for Jake's boot heels to DRAG and BOUNCE across the desert floor -- he holds on through gritted teeth, but then SEES:

ELLA! Clamped under the wing -- SHOCKED to see him dragging behind the speeder -- and this gives him STRENGTH, he SWINGS an arm up, pulling his upper torso onto the wing -- now the rest of him -- his weight causes the ship to TILT VERTICALLY --

Jake's holding on upright to the speeder now, as if scaling the side of a moving train -- the ship slots into a NARROWER PART OF THE CANYON and TILTS HORIZONTAL AGAIN --

He LOSES his grip -- catches the EDGE of the wing -- ON JAKE -- Realizing he can shift the craft's weight --

HIS POV -- he SEES Ella through the wing's SLATS -- climbs back up -- reaching for her BINDS -- starts PULLING her free --

UP AHEAD -- A SMALL LAKE

EXT. A SMALL LAKE - DAY

In the middle of the desert. ON JAKE -- As he gets an IDEA:

> JAKE
>
> GIMME YOUR HAND!!!

-- She REACHES for him -- their hands CLASP -- he PULLS, her binds GIVING WAY -- as Jake reaches up between the wing and TAKES HOLD -- PULLING DOWN -- the crafts starts to ANGLE DOWNWARD . . . TOWARD THE LAKE:

> ELLA
>
> WHAT'RE YOU DOING?!

HOLD ON!!!!

-- The craft SCREAMS DOWN TOWARD THE WATER -- Jake PULLS HARD and Ella finally BREAKS LOOSE --

JAKE AND ELLA FALL INTO THE WATER AS THE SPEEDER CRASHES, SKIMMING THE SURFACE, THEN SPIRALING DOWN, KICKING UP A GEYSER OF SPRAY!

A beat -- then PUUUUUH!!!!! Jake and Ella break the surface. Bruised but very much ALIVE:

EXT. LAKE SHORE - DAY

They stagger up onto the bank. Breathing. Looking at each other. He SMILES. So does she. Giddy --

                    JAKE
              (catching his breath)
          We . . . were . . . flying . . .

                    ELLA
          Yeah, we were . . .

                    JAKE
          I don't wanna do that again.

Their eyes MEET. Her clothes cling to her body in a way that can't be ignored. As their faces seem to INCH CLOSER . . .

A GLISTENING SHAPE rises up from the water behind them. Dripping, TERRIFYING -- Jake turns, it STRIKES -- Ella SCREAMS -- Jake's blaster OPENS and FIRES -- <u>BLASTING THE CREATURE TO BITS</u>.

Holy shit. A GURGLE/GASP -- Jake turns -- ELLA, on the ground, chest BLOODY. The alien PIERCED HER with its claw:

                    JAKE (CONT'D)
          -- No --

-- He cradles her head -- she looks up at him -- bewildered, in pain -- he gently rocks her, brushing a strand of hair off her forehead:

                         JAKE (CONT'D)
          Ella, Ella -- c'mon, talk to me --

Her eyes fight to focus on him -- blinking --

                            ELLA
          -- Don't worry. I'm gonna be okay.

                            JAKE
          We're gonna find Doc --

                            ELLA
          I'll be -- alright -- just go --

Jake staggers to his feet, Ella in his arms. Starts CARRYING HER back in the direction they came from and . . .

EXT. DESERT PLAINS - LATER

HEAT SHIMMERS off the desert. Jake appears as a SPECK coming over dunes, carrying Ella under the merciless sun. No man can live long in this heat. He looks down at her chalk-white face:

                            JAKE
          Hey. Stay with me.

Her lids open, close lazily again . . . seemingly on the verge of death . . . but she can read him, sees it in his eyes . . .

                            ELLA
          You remember now . . . don't you . . .

                            JAKE
          . . . what?

                            ELLA
          The woman.

Jake stares off . . . he has the puzzle pieces, but still doesn't know what the picture's supposed to look like . . .

> ELLA (CONT'D)
> Did you love her?

No answer . . .

> ELLA (CONT'D)
> You can tell me . . .

> JAKE
> (a beat)
> I guess I must've.
> (beat)
> It's just . . . hard to see . . .
> (beat)
> All I know is . . . I owe it to her to find her.

He stumbles on. She looks at him, fading . . . fatigue and delirium are starting to take hold of him too . . .

> JAKE (CONT'D)
> . . . it's not far . . . you hang in there . . . hang . . . in . . . we're gonna be fine . . .

Off that --

EXT. ROCKY HILLS - DAY

A HORSE trotting along, then another . . . DOLARHYDE, EMMETT, followed by DOC and COLORADO . . . having survived the alien attack, dusty as hell, WALKING THEIR HORSES. A sense they've LOST so much now. Doc looks to Colorado:

> DOC
> This plan wasn't very well thought out, was it?
> (no response)
> We lost?

> NAT COLORADO
> We'll be all right.

                              DOC
     How can you be so <u>calm</u> in all this? I
     nearly messed my britches.

                         NAT COLORADO
             (a beat)
     You were good back there. Held your own
     with the gang. Rode hard just now. We
     survived a battle together. Look at you,
     you're a warrior now. Your wife won't
     even recognize you when you see her.

                              DOC
             (defeated)
     <u>If</u> I see her . . .

And Nat looks right at Doc, means it when he says:

                         NAT COLORADO
     In Apache, there is no word for goodbye.

Doc takes that in. An odd comfort.

ANOTHER ANGLE -- DOLARHYDE AND EMMETT, side by side. The
kid's been crying, trying not to let anyone see:

                         DOLARHYDE
     What're you all bunched up about?

Emmett wipes his nose, sniffles:

                            EMMETT
     . . . I miss my grandpa.

Dolarhyde considers the kid.

                         DOLARHYDE
     I wasn't much older than you, back when
     this territory was Mexico. Word come,
     Apaches were headed for a settlement
     outside Arivaca. My father wanted me to
     be a man, so he made me ride out with the
     garrison, banging on a drum. Boy, was I
     scared.

Emmett looks up at Dolarhyde. A kind gesture to admit that.

                              DOLARHYDE (CONT'D)
              So when we got to Arivaca, found the
              whole place burned to the ground. Then
              I saw a settler crawling from a cabin
              that caught fire . . . he was burnt bad
              -- knew he was dyin'. All he could manage
              was two words:
                       (beat)
              "Kill me."

Emmett stares, wide eyed, rapt:

                              EMMETT
              . . . what'd you do?

Dolarhyde pulls the KNIFE he gave him from off Emmett's
belt:

                              DOLARHYDE
              I took this very knife . . . and I slit
              his throat.

Dolarhyde SPINS the knife in his hand, holds it out for
Emmett, who stares, jarred at the history of the gleaming
blade he's been carrying. Then . . . in a real first,
Dolarhyde puts a comforting hand on Emmett's shoulder --
softly:

                              DOLARHYDE (CONT'D)
              Now be a man.

ON EMMETT -- Empowered through his fear . . .

                              NAT COLORADO
              Boss, look!

Up ahead, they spot the outline of Jake carrying Ella.

EXT. ROCKY HILLS - SUNSET

      INTO FRAME COMES JAKE -- lips cracked, can't even talk, all
      he can do is utter HOARSE, RASPY MOANS. We can't tell if

Ella's alive or dead by now. And then -- he STOPS. Because he SEES:

Dolarhyde, Nat, Doc, and Emmett on the horizon. Jake squints -- is it a mirage?

JAKE

> H -- he -- here -- we -- we made it --

He COLLAPSES to his knees. The rest of our people REAR and DISMOUNT. Dolarhyde scans the hills with URGENT CONCERN as Doc TAKES HOLD of Ella:

DOC

> Give her to me --

As Dolarhyde offers his canteen to Jake:

JAKE

> Her f-first --

-- Doc tends to Ella, feels her vitals, but she's LIMP --

A beat: Doc glances up at Dolarhyde with that awful "she's dead" look. ON DOLARHYDE -- Unexpectedly STRUCK. He's feeling it. For the first time, we see what passes for COMPASSION as he ACTIVATES. Tries to get Jake to stand --

JAKE (CONT'D)

> -- how is she?

DOLARHYDE

> She's gone.

JAKE

> She's not gone. Lemme see her --

Dolarhyde looks at him -- HARD:

DOLARHYDE

> Jake . . . she's gone.

NAT COLORADO

> Boss.

Dolarhyde looks up -- the Apaches are <u>all around them</u> on the ridge. BOWS DRAWN, FIERCE. OUR PEOPLE ARE SURROUNDED. Off this:

EXT. NEW MEXICO MOUNTAINS - TWILIGHT

The sun DIPS behind the mountains . . . NIGHT FALLS . . .

EXT. APACHE CAMP - NIGHT

CHAOS AND CONFUSION, SHOUTING -- Jake is DROPPED in the dirt, MUMBLING incoherently.

Dolarhyde, Nat, and Doc are pushed to their knees by APACHE WARRIORS.

ON EMMETT -- Terrified, held away from the men. Other Apaches sort through our crew's RIFLES and GUNS, showing them to a wizened SACHEM (Black Knife) sitting on a raised platform -- he gestures to a Warrior who YELLS at Colorado -- Colorado ARGUES BACK in Apache, translating as Dolarhyde BARKS over him --

NAT COLORADO	**DOLARHYDE**
He says this is all	
that's left of their	
clans -- the Western	-- <u>Sonsabitches</u> --
Apache, Chiricahua, and	-- who gives a <u>shit</u> --
Mescalero -- they all	don't even listen to 'em,
came here, they lost	there's no reason, we're
people too --	all <u>dead</u> --

Dolarhyde keeps his eyes LOCKED on Black Knife --

> **NAT COLORADO**
> -- he says the White Man brought bad
> medicine to his people the last fifty
> years -- diseases, plague -- and now
> we brought the Wind Walkers -- that we
> burned their people.

In retaliation, Ella's BODY is thrown into a BONFIRE in the center of camp -- <u>she starts to burn</u>.

                              EMMETT
          NOOO!!!

                               DOC
          -- what? He thinks we did that?! They're
          takin' our people too! Just tell 'em!!

                            DOLARHYDE
          Forget it. Ain't no reasoning with 'em.

Colorado repeats the plea but it's a LOSING DEBATE --
they're all YANKED UP by their hair, JAKE too -- jarring
him back to half-consciousness -- as he watches Ella's
body burn.

                              JAKE
          Stop --

Black Knife stares, deciding the fates of our people. ON
DOLARHYDE -- Eyes blazing HATE:

                            DOLARHYDE
          Kill us now, GET IT DONE WITH!!

WHACK! Dolarhyde is CLUBBED by the butt of a tomahawk as
Black Knife NODS: "death." KNIVES are pressed to throats
-- Emmett tries to break free and run toward his people,
but he's HELD BACK, tears streaming, shouting "NONONO!!"
-- and just before their throats are slit:

FWOOM! THE PYRE SUDDENLY BILLOWS, TURNING FROM ORANGE TO
GREEN TO WHITE -- EVERYONE BACKS AWAY AS --

ELLA EMERGES FROM THE PYRE WRAPPED IN A CAUL OF FIRE AND
LIGHT!

Except she isn't exactly Ella. She's a HUMANOID LIGHT
BEING, radiating a blinding, angelic glow.

Yeah, Ella's an alien.

PANDEMONIUM. The Apache kneel in prostration, DROPPING
weapons as flames DISSIPATE off her backlit form. With each
step, her skin RETURNS to human flesh tone. Hair too. When
she finally STOPS, she looks like the woman we know. Alive.

FIFTY DUMBSTRUCK FACES stare at her.

ON JAKE -- NOW he's sure as hell AWAKE. Doesn't know what's happening . . . but his heart is suddenly, unexpectedly FULL.

Ella stands there. A strange expression on her face.

Jake staggers up. Looks at her. Doesn't know <u>what</u> to say. Pulls a BLANKET off the ground . . . moves to her . . . WRAPS her in it. Steps back. She looks at him, regretful:

>   ELLA
>   I couldn't tell you.

After a beat he speaks, sotto:

>   JAKE
>   Are you one of them?

>   ELLA
>   No. I'm from a different place.
>   (beat)
>   I took this form . . . so I could walk
>   among you.

>   JAKE
>   You should've told me.

>   ELLA
>   I didn't know if I could heal this body.
>   If I would wake up.

He just looks at her -- words that don't compute. Black Knife SPEAKS, gestures toward a thatched hut:

>   NAT COLORADO
>   (translating)
>   He invites you into the Tent Of Meeting.

Everyone looks at the tent. Off that --

EXT. APACHE CAMP - NIGHT

FIRELIGHT behind hanging ANIMAL-HIDE SKINS, draped from beech-bark poles . . . we SLOW TRACK around them to see, in IMPRESSIONS: Ella slipping a cotton shirt over her body . . . a pair of MEN'S JEANS are removed from one of the guys' saddlebags. She steps out from behind the skins . . .

INT. HUT - TALKING CIRCLE - NIGHT

Black Knife and a few braves sit, watching Ella with REVERENCE. AWE. On the other side (detente, for now) are Dolarhyde, Colorado, Jake, Doc, Emmett. Black Knife speaks; Nat translates:

> NAT COLORADO
> Where are you from?

Ella looks to Black Knife, and then, amazingly, she answers him in PERFECT APACHE. Looks up to the stars -- a measure of sadness as she speaks. Dolarhyde leans into Colorado:

> DOLARHYDE
> The hell's she saying?

> NAT COLORADO
> That she comes from a place above the stars. Another world.

Everyone takes this in. Dolarhyde isn't having it:

> DOLARHYDE
> Another world?

> NAT COLORADO
> And that if we work together, we can get our people back.

> DOLARHYDE
> "Work" with them?

Black Knife GLARES at the interruption, speaks ANGRILY --

NAT COLORADO	DOLARHYDE
You -- you shouldn't talk --	-- why the hell shouldn't I talk?! I got questions too --
-- it's an insult, a guest of the chief's must be invited to speak --	-- oh, am I a guest now? Or am I a prisoner? What the hell am I?

Black Knife points at Dolarhyde, SHOUTING reaches a FEVER PITCH-

                              DOC
          HEY! Enough! You're both big men, all
          right? Greeeat warriors! Can we just
          listen to the woman tell her story? Or
          -- whatever the hell she is.

                              JAKE
          What do they want?

                              ELLA
          They want gold. It's as rare to them as
          it is to you.

ON JAKE, as it starts to PENETRATE. The aliens came to his cabin . . . for GOLD. Long beat -- Dolarhyde sort of CHUCKLES:

                         DOLARHYDE
          Well that's just -- ridiculous. What're
          they gonna do, buy something?

                              DOC
          Is Maria alive? The others?

Everyone shares a look. Finally:

                              ELLA
          If they are, they won't be for long.

As the horrible chill of that lands . . .

ELLA (CONT'D)

They're learning your weaknesses.
> (beat)

It's what they did to my people. First
one ship came, then more. We fought back
. . . but they were stronger. Only a few
of us escaped.

PAIN in her eyes -- but also, URGENCY:

ELLA (CONT'D)

I came here to stop them from doing
it again. But we have to move quickly
. . . before they leave and bring back
others.

Beat. Black Knife speaks to Ella.

ELLA (CONT'D)
> (as Black Knife keeps speaking)

He says his men will follow me.

DOLARHYDE

Wait a minute, slow down -- what the
hell you mean, you're gonna "follow her"?
Where're you gonna go? What're you gonna
do?

ELLA
> (indicates Jake)

He's the only one who knows where they
are. You've been there.

Jake shakes his head, struggling . . .

JAKE

I couldn't even remember my name. If it's
in here? I can't get it out.

Black Knife and his men CONFER, look to Jake and speak.

ELLA

They say they have medicine that will
heal your memories.

Sound of CHANTING takes us to:

EXT. THATCHED HUT - LATER - NIGHT

A STONE MORTAR filled with some kind of BROWN LIQUID is
passed from hand to hand. It's finally handed to JAKE.

He stares at the foul liquid -- SNIFFS -- ugh -- looks at
Ella:

                         ELLA
           . . . please.

Softly. Needing him to do this. He glances around at the
other faces -- their hopes all pinned to him.

                         DOC
           Hell, worth a try. Can't be any worse
           than the snake oil I serve.

Finally, he shakes his head . . . and DRINKS.

Several Apaches start leading Jake and Ella into the Wikiup
-- others hold out hands to tell Dolarhyde, Doc, Emmett:
"Stay here." They trade concerned looks as --

INT. WIKIUP - NIGHT

Suddenly, the drug takes effect and Jake's face becomes
placid, his eyes widen. Ella lowers him back, leaning over
him . . . he looks at her, drowsy . . . the fire casts her
in ethereal light . . .

   . . . A HUMMINGBIRD flutters into the tent, ZIG-ZAGS over
Jake. The Apache take note, recognizing the sacred omen as
a positive one: Jake's animal guide. Now the scene BLURS
out of focus . . . then BLURS BACK . . .

EXT. DESERT DUNES - DAY

And it's ALICE. What? She's MOVING -- through DESERT DUNES
-- where are we? The billowing sands growing WILDER, harder
to see her through -- as she turns back to us with loving
eyes:

                         ALICE
           . . . it's not your fault . . .

ON JAKE -- He says "What?" -- but NO SOUND comes out of his mouth . . . as we CUT TO:

INT. THATCHED HUT - DAY

Ella stroking Jake's hair. His eyes still closed, only the Apaches gathered around:

EXT. DUNES - DAY

The sound of WHIRLING SAND overtakes the soundtrack as Jake stammers on through the dunes, looking for Alice -- CALLS OUT:

JAKE

   . . . hello?!

INT. THATCHED HUT - NIGHT

In his drugged state, Jake WHISPERS:

JAKE

   . . . hello . . .

Ella's eyes close . . . <u>CONNECTING with him</u>:

EXT. DUNES - DAY

The sandstorm OBSCURES FRAME -- we've lost Alice now, though her voice ECHOES:

ALICE

 . . . it's not your fault . . .

Jake turns, and THERE she is -- moving to him -- so beautiful -- and they KISS. As they do, we <u>TUMBLE INTO ANOTHER ENVIRONMENT</u>:

EXT. JAKE'S CABIN - COTTONWOOD GROVE - DAY

WAVING GRASS. The plains somewhere. As we RISE UP to reveal . . . we're in front of the cabin. DARK SKIES overhead -- A FLASH OF LIGHT and suddenly Jake finds himself:

INT. JAKE'S CABIN - DAY

> INSIDE -- _as we replay the moment WE SAW earlier, but now_
> _we play it out in full_ -- as Jake drops his SADDLEBAG on
> the cabin table with a CLINK. She pulls away from him, her
> face darkening:

> > > > ALICE
> > > -- Where'd you get that?

> > > > JAKE
> > > Where do you think?

> > > > ALICE
> > > Take it back.

> And this goes from zero-to-sixty FAST:

> > > JAKE   ALICE
> > Like hell --   -- that's blood money --

> > -- it's gonna buy us   -- by robbin' and
> > what we need, I goddamned killin', _this ain't a_
> > earned_ it --   _clean break_. Don't you
> >   understand?

> And suddenly, a RUMBLE interrupts the argument -- Jake's
> SADDLEBAG tumbles over and . . . GOLD COINS clink out,
> spilling across the floor. We know what comes next --

INT. THATCHED HUT - NIGHT

> Jake starts to TWITCH violently -- his pores IGNITE in
> sweat:

> > > > JAKE
> > > -- NO --

> ON ELLA -- _Feeling what he feels_ . . .

INT. JAKE'S CABIN - DAY

> **BAM!** _LIGHT BLASTS DOWN FROM ABOVE!_ Alice SCREAMS as she's
> pulled up into the light -- then . . . FROM JAKE'S POV, A

BOLO COMES AT US -- WRAPS AROUND US -- WE ARE RAISED INTO
THE LIGHT, and we WHITEWASH TO:

INT. CAVERN - DAY

STACCATO FLASHING LIGHT -- (same images from our opening)
-- blurred, violent images: SOMEPLACE VERY DARK AND SCARY
-- WE'RE IN A CAVE NOW: ZOMBIELIKE HUMAN FACES STARING UP
AT THAT STACCATO FLASHING LIGHT --

FLASHCUT: Now we're being strapped onto the most TERRIFYING
TABLE IMAGINABLE by an ALIEN looming above us -- POV WHIPS
LEFT, RIGHT -- RESTRAINING CLAMPS ENFOLD OUR SKULL -- but
we manage to see:

INT. CAVERN LAB - DAY

ALICE. On another OPERATING TABLE beside him. Lying in the
same position she was in on the grass -- and she's NOT
moving:

                         JAKE
              . . . Alice . . . Alice!!!!

ANOTHER ALIEN is operating on her --

INT. THATCHED HUT - NIGHT

Jake SCREAMS and thrashes --

ON ELLA, feeling it too -- TEARS in her eyes as:

INT. CAVERN LAB - DAY

ALICE -- BLOOD is seeping through her dress, across her
CHEST. We do not see, but it's implied, she's been torn
open. And yeah, she's very, very DEAD.

Jake STRUGGLES, but those BINDS keep him down. The alien
looming over him readies some horrifying OPERATING TOOLS.

CLOSE -- ITS EYES BULGE, studying Jake like he's a fly in
a web.

A THIN LASER starts CUTTING into Jake's chest -- the very
wound Jake woke up with in the desert --

As Jake SCREAMS in pain, the adrenaline surge allows his hand to BREAK FREE from the strap --

INT. CAVERN LAB - DAY

-- Jake's free hand -- thrashing for something -- anything -- grabs a METAL OBJECT off a tray near the table -- and to his surprise . . . it RESPONDS like a live thing, COILING AROUND HIS WRIST! A BLASTER BRACELET. **BLAM!**

The alien above him MOVES to avoid the hit, but the laser SHREDS HIS FACE . . . LEAVING A RED SCAR. Holy shit, this is Red Scar! It was Jake who gave the creature its wound --

The alien near Alice SCREECHES but Jake FIRES at it, BLASTING THE ALIEN INTO OBLIVION -- Jake rips the other straps off --

One last, awful look at Alice, and now we're RUNNING, ESCAPE:

INT. CAVERN TUNNELS - DAY

Through cavern tunnels -- left -- right -- POV BLURRY -- strange ALIEN STRUTS reinforce the walls -- LIGHT ahead and suddenly --

EXT. ROCK FORMATION - SAME

WHAM! We're OUTSIDE -- looking up at a strange ROCK FORMATION on the cliffs high above.

Like a STONE TOWER pointing to heaven -- the CACOPHONY OF SOUNDS reaches a CRESCENDO and:

INT. THATCHED HUT - CONTINUOUS

JAKE GASPS BACK TO CONSCIOUSNESS, like emerging from the ocean depths, overcome with the pain of his returned memory. Ella holds him --

JAKE
(choking back the shock)
I brought the gold . . . in the house .
. . that's why she's dead.

                              ELLA
                    (holding him tighter)
              It's not your fault.

ON JAKE -- Little comfort there. But something else, too
. . .

                              JAKE
              I know where they are . . .

EXT. ROCKS NEAR SHIP - DAY

THE SAME ROCK FROM HIS MEMORY APPEARS ON A BLUFF AHEAD.

Jake and Dolarhyde, leading our group, enter frame as they
climb to a vantage point overlooking a rocky valley below.

Black Knife and several of his warriors approach with them.
As they reach the top, we RISE ABOVE THEM to see what they
see:

A CYLINDRICAL FREIGHTER, A MONOLITH OF ALIEN STEEL. Ugly
and battered, like a massive tombstone, jutting out from
the ground.

SHOCK -- their minds BEND. Never in their lives have they
seen anything like it . . . Dolarhyde raises his Scope to
peer at the ship.

POV - THROUGH A SPYGLASS - THE ALIEN SHIP

                         DOLARHYDE
              Jesus, Mary, an' Joseph . . . how'd they
              . . . build something like that?

ON ELLA -- Lit with PURPOSE. Her whole mission has been
leading up to this:

                              ELLA
              They came here in it. That's only the top
              . . . the rest is underground.
                         (beat)
              It's how they mine for gold.

                    DOLARHYDE
Can they see outta that thing?

                      ELLA
It's hard for them to see in the daylight.
They stay below ground, where it's dark.

WHOOSH! A speeder ROARS right over them, dipping into the
canyon. They crouch lower to avoid being seen, watching as
the speeder slots into a LANDING PORT at the top of the
tower . . .

                      DOC
We'll never even get close. Those flying
machines'll just pick us off before we
get anywhere near it.

                      JAKE
There's another way underground.
        (beat)
  -- the same way I got out.

                    DOLARHYDE
That's an impenetrable fort. We gotta
draw those things out and fight 'em in
the open, distract 'em so you can get
inside with that arm gun and get our
people out.

                      ELLA
We have one advantage. They underestimate
you -- you're like insects to them.
They're not planning on defending
themselves, so they'll be vulnerable.

                    DOLARHYDE
        (beat, realizing)
We don't have the manpower or the
ordinance.

ON JAKE -- Mind turning quickly.

                                    JAKE
                        This is not gonna work.

Black Knife speaks; Nat translates --

                              NAT COLORADO
                        He wants to use your spy glass.

Dolarhyde throws Black Knife a skeptical look. Share? Black
Knife stares back. Finally, Dolarhyde gives him the device,
but his face tells us he knows the odds are bad.

Black Knife peers at the ship, then at the ridges
surrounding it. He speaks, Nat translates:

                          NAT COLORADO (CONT'D)
                        The Apache are mountain warriors. He says
                        it's better to fight from high ground.

                              DOLARHYDE
                        Tell him he's a fool if he thinks we can
                        shoot a few arrows from on high and hurt
                        these things.

But before Nat can translate:

                                  EMMETT
                              (then, realizing)
                        Where's Jake?

The others turn, only now noticing that Jake is gone. And
then they see, far below, JAKE IS ALREADY RIDING AWAY.
Leaving them there.

ON ELLA -- REACTING -- Is he leaving for good? As Doc says:

                                  DOC
                        Well, that's just <u>great</u>.

                              DOLARHYDE
                        . . . goddamn coward . . .

                                  DOC
                        What did you say to him this time?

EXT. DESERT PLAINS - DAY

Jake gallops through the desert, fast -- RIGHT INTO FRAME:

EXT. DESERT - ESTABLISHING - DAY

Jake rides alone through plains . . .

EXT. JAKE'S GANG ENCAMPMENT - DAY

What remains of JAKE'S GANG -- roughly 20 of them -- tend wounds after the speeder attack. All shell shocked. Bronc, on his knees, counts the gold they have left as Hunt looks on. BULL, now in charge, hovers over them both.

> **BULL**
> (to Bronc)
> Quit stalling -- how much gold we got left?

> **BRONC**
> Okay, *calmate . . . como cincuenta pedasos* --
> (calculating)
> -- a thousand dollars, maybe more.

> **HUNT**
> (on edge)
> Just need to know how much of that is mine, and I'll be on my way.

> **BULL**
> On your way? Dolan's dead, so I run this gang now --
> (beat)
> Gold goes where I go.

But Hunt is fast, pulls his gun in a blink.

> **HUNT**
> You might be in charge, but some of that gold is mine fair. And after what we saw today, I need it to get as far from here as I can go.

Now all the men raise their guns, taking one side or the other.

BULL

You're not going anywhere.

Bronc finally stands to break the tie, pistol pointed at Bull.

BRONC

Perdoname. What's fair is fair.

Suddenly, on the horizon against the SUN -- a LONE RIDER approaches. Dismounts. JAKE. He walks right into camp. TENSION . . .

WHAT'S HE DOING HERE? Is he here to kill them, or help them?

A WHINE brings Jake's attention to . . . THE DOG. Having found its way to the camp. Trots up to Jake, tail wagging. He stares at the dog, pleasantly surprised -- chuckles:

JAKE

Where you been?

HUNT

Jake? That really you?

Jake casually takes a seat on a nearby rock.

JAKE

You boys thinking of taking a trip?

BRONC

Patron, we're thinking of riding south. Remember the playa in Puerto Vallarta?

HUNT

Yeah, tequila, good fishing.

JAKE

Not far enough.

                              HUNT

        Jake, what the hell were those things?

                              JAKE

        Don't matter. They're gonna find us.

                              HUNT

          . . . the hell're you saying?

                              JAKE

        I'm saying you got a choice. You can
        drink your last few hours away on a
        beach, which is not a bad idea, by the
        way . . .
                    (beat)
        Or you can follow me one last time.

Uneasy glances all around: <u>follow him</u>?

                              BULL

        Why the hell would we do that?

                              JAKE

        Same reason you always have . . .
                    (a wry grin)
        . . . because I'll make you rich.

Oh. <u>That's</u> a word they understand. Off the twinkle in
Jake's eye --

EXT. APACHE CAMP - DAY

BANG! Find Doc firing off the last round or two of his rifle
. . . a satisfied look on his face marks his progress.

Just then, his attention turns toward the camp as an
argument escalates: Dolarhyde trying and failing to engage
Black Knife in a STRATEGY SESSION. Ella translating:

                            DOLARHYDE

        <u>Listen to me!</u>

Black Knife stops now, as all his braves look on at the
sound of Dolarhyde raising his voice --

DOLARHYDE (CONT'D)

We can't just run around hooting and
throwing spears at that damn thing! Tell
him we gotta find a way to bring 'em out
onto open ground . . . then hit 'em from
all sides, FLANK THEM!

Black Knife speaks.

ELLA

He says yours is not the voice of wisdom.
He won't let you lead his people in
battle.

As Black Knife's anger ESCALATES, we go CLOSE on Nat --
reaching a BREAKING POINT -- until finally, he SHOUTS:

NAT COLORADO
(at Black Knife)
ENOUGH!

All eyes fall on Nat, as he speaks with FORCE to Black
Knife -- and though we can't understand him, we feel his
PASSION:

DOLARHYDE
(sotto: to Ella)
What's he saying . . .?

Ella and Dolarhyde, CLOSE:

ELLA

He says they have to open their eyes to
see in you what he's seen . . . that his
parents were killed in the Mexican War,
and you took him in when he was only a
boy . . .

And as she repeats, ELLA's AFFECTED by what she's repeating
. . . a revelation to her, to us . . .

                              ELLA (CONT'D)
          . . . you gave a purpose, taught him how
          to take care of himself. Even though you
          didn't share the same blood.

ON DOLARHYDE -- Though he's trying not to be, he's MOVED.
That stoic veneer quickly starting to crack . . .

                              ELLA (CONT'D)
          And that you despise battle, but never
          run from it.
                    (beat)
          That you are a great warrior . . . worthy
          of any fight.

And now, Dolarhyde and Nat meet eyes. An incredible moment
passes between them -- it's all in the SILENCE, but the
connection between these men is POWERFULLY FELT. Finally,
Black Knife speaks, still challenging, though clearly Nat's
words have made an impression . . .

                              ELLA (CONT'D)
          He says if you're such a great warrior,
          how come you don't have men to fight by
          your side?

Their look HOLDS -- then, COMMOTION. Some Apaches have
spotted . . . JAKE in the distance, trotting over the
plains. Alone. Then . . .

HIS GANG RISES INTO VIEW BEHIND HIM, TWENTY MORE MEN COMING
OVER, THE HILL. A MOMENT OF PERFECT TIMING, AND VICTORY.

CLOSE ON THE FACES OF OUR PEOPLE. THIS CHANGES THE TIDE.

ON EMMETT -- As he sees the dog trotting alongside Jake's
horse. It RUNS downhill to him, leaps on the boy who drops
to grab him:

                              EMMETT
          Hi, Boy!!!

As Jake dismounts, Emmett rushes up and HUGS him.

It's AWKWARD -- as we're ON JAKE, unaccustomed to this kind of affection, especially from a child. He sort of half smiles, as he edges the boy off . . .

                    JAKE
          Okay, Kid.

And now he meets eyes with Dolarhyde. And God DAMN if we don't love these two together by now. As Jake walks right up to the rancher, the man stand eye to eye -- for the first time, PARTNERS instead of ADVERSARIES:

                    JAKE (CONT'D)
          I got an idea how to take out those
          flyers, draw 'em out . . .
                    (beat)
          You ready to get your son back?

ON DOLARHYDE -- Hell yes.

ON BLACK KNIFE -- Watching. As Dolarhyde looks to him. The two men lock eyes . . . then finally, Black Knife NODS and our MUSIC GOES INTO FULL UPSWING:

As we begin the sound of BEATING DRUMS:

EXT. APACHE CAMP/COWBOY CAMP - DAY

The sound of the Apache drums performing a ceremonial war dance in the neighboring camp permeates the following vignettes:

COWBOY'S CAMP -- our men are gathered around a couple of small campfires in the night. We find Hunt sitting next to Bull and Red as Dolarhyde walks by, surveying his troops --

                    HUNT
          -- Dolarhyde.

Dolarhyde stops, turns toward Hunt.

                    HUNT (CONT'D)
          You the same Colonel Woodrow Dolarhyde
          who fought at Antietam?

Beat -- is Dolarhyde gonna tear his head off?

                    DOLARHYDE
              (accepting the fact that:)
         Yes I am.

Dolarhyde moves off, toward the growing sound of:

TRADITIONAL APACHE WAR DANCE -- BLACK KNIFE PRESIDING

Dolarhyde watches them for a beat. Jake approaches, the two
men now standing side by side. A long beat before:

                  DOLARHYDE (CONT'D)
         I knew you'd be back.

And the way he says it is almost warm. Dolarhyde turns and
walks back into the night.

                      JAKE
              (quietly to himself)
         You're welcome.

ANOTHER ANGLE -- ON EMMETT, watching the Apache war dance
from a hidden vantage point. Colorado appears behind him.

                  NAT COLORADO
         Hey, Emmett, you shouldn't be here.

Emmett shuffles off. Nat's about to follow when he notices
Black Knife's spotted him. They share a look, and then,
to Colorado's surprise, Black Knife gestures him over to a
seat next to him by the fire. For Colorado, a major moment
in his life, a part of his soul has been given acceptance.
Colorado moves toward his people and sits next to Black
Knife.

                  BLACK KNIFE
              (in Apache)
         You are a good Apache.

With that, Black Knife stands and joins the dance, leaving
Colorado to watch a celebration of the life he never knew.

ANOTHER ANGLE -- ELLA -- LOOKING UP AT THE STARS

-- Jake appears behind her.

                        ELLA
            Just so you know, I'm not going to be
            here for very long.

                        JAKE
            None of us are here for very long.

Jake takes his hat off and kisses Ella.

                    JAKE (CONT'D)
            Don't ever do that to me again.

MUSIC SOARS and we --

EXT. HILLS NEAR APACHE CAMP - DAY

Our cavalry rides out toward their final battle -- an
impressive stampede of men and horses.

They slow as they crest a hill, cowboys and Apaches,
side by side but not yet fully united. They trade looks,
acknowledging their mutual need despite their misgivings.

EXT. ARRIVAL AT PLAZA BLANCA - DAY

Our cavalry rides into the hostile terrain. As they reach
a fork in the rocks, Black Knife leads his warriors up the
higher trail while Jake and Dolarhyde lead the others into
the arroyo.

The two groups part ways, eyeing each other suspiciously
as they split.

EXT. CANYON - NEAR ALIEN SHIP - DAY

WE are GLIDING HIGH over the canyon bluff to reveal the
ALIEN SHIP, looming dark and silent, pressed into the
ground . . . we DIP LOWER to find:

JAKE + A FEW GANG MEMBERS creeping toward the base of the
ship.

EXT. ROCKS ABOVE BATTLEFIELD - DAY

BEHIND A RIDGE -- THE REST OF OUR HEROES WATCH FROM THEIR
PERCH: DOLARHYDE, ELLA, COLORADO, DOC and EMMETT.

                         DOLARHYDE
          There they go.

EXT. ROCKS ABOVE SLOT CANYON - APACHE

Black Knife leads his warriors into position. They, too,
witness Jake and his gang as they approach the tower.

JAKE'S POV

As he leads his men toward the ship, he stops to survey his
surroundings. He sees, on the rocks above the slot canyon,
Black Knife leading his tribe into position, the Apache
seemingly disappearing into the mountainside. Jake and his
men press on . . .

EXT. ALIEN SHIP - DAY

Jake and his men reach the base and begin to climb.

Once Jake is halfway up the side of the ship, Jake gives
hand signals and A SATCHEL OF DYNAMITE is passed up to
Jake. He slips it into OPEN VENTS on the speeder port.
Fuses are threaded and set, but before they can light them,
one of his men fumbles with the MATCHES and drops them!
Jake gestures toward Bronc, who chomps on a lit cigar --
Bronc passes the cigar up to Jake, who uses it to LIGHT
THE FUSE.

TELESCOPE POV -- the men in position, climbing up, waiting,
beginning their climb down. POV WHIPS UP to the SPEEDER
PORT on top of the ship. Through the open bay doors,
SPEEDERS inside. NO ALIENS IN SIGHT.

BACK TO SCENE: The men quickly start climbing DOWN the side
of the ship as the fuses BURN. As the men reach the bottom
and RUN, flame meets dynamite and BA-BOOM! The speeders
DETONATE in a cloud of fire and shrapnel.

JAKE AND THE MEN -- RUNNING -- WHOOPS of victory, but then -- the detonation sets off a series of BIGGER, TERTIARY EXPLOSIONS that lick out the ship's vents -- the men are nearly knocked off their feet by the blast --

ON JAKE, TURNING -- senses what's about to happen next:

SAME, DOLARHYDE, AND ELLA -- and here it comes:

IRISES OPEN ON THE SHIP AND ALIENS STREAM OUT, FIRING MEGA-PULSES AT JAKE AND THE FLEEING MEN. A HORNET'S NEST.

EXT. ALIEN SHIP - DAY

ALIEN POV -- under cranked and blown out, we see what the aliens see as they chase Jake and his men, firing blasters.

EXT. ROCKS ABOVE BATTLEFIELD - CONTINUOUS

NAT COLORADO
They're coming out.

DOLARHYDE
Let's move --

The group starts to move -- Dolarhyde turns to Emmett, hands him the telescope:

DOLARHYDE
Take this, go up where I showed you. If you see our people come out, get up and wave your arms.

As Dolarhyde moves off, EMMETT scuttles up onto the RIDGE. The dog sticks close as the kid scans the field through the TELESCOPE --

EXT. FOOT OF ROCKY LOOKOUT/EDGE OF BATTLEFIELD - CONTINUOUS

Jake and his men round the corner, finally getting out of the line of fire. They find half the men already on horseback awaiting orders as Dolarhyde and Ella descend from the lookout above.

                              JAKE
          They're all yours.

                            DOLARHYDE
          Good job.

A final look between the two men. This is it.

                              JAKE
             If they're in there, we'll get 'em out.

Jake and Ella ready their weapons.

                            DOLARHYDE
          Godspeed.

Jake and Ella move off toward the slot canyon, crossing Doc
as he pulls his medical kit from his saddlebags.

Dolarhyde mounts up -- steels himself a beat before:

                       DOLARHYDE (CONT'D)
             Let's go!

A dozen horsemen follow Dolarhyde's charge --

EXT. FOOT OF ROCKY LOOKOUT/OTHER SIDE OF BATTLEFIELD - DAY

     Nat arrives to another contingent of cowboys, the other
     half of Jake's gang, also mounted up and ready to follow
     Nat into battle. Nat climbs onto his horse -- and they're
     off!

EXT. BATTLEFIELD - DAY

     Thundering hooves fill the canyon floor:

     THE FIRST WAVE OF MEN CHARGES IN ON HORSEBACK LED BY
     DOLARHYDE, all firing!

     Across the battlefield, Nat leads his men in the flanking
     maneuver. Both sides zeroing in on the alien front.

     An alien fires his blaster and blows one of the men off his
     horse. Another man is SWIPED off of his horse by the alien

as they pass it. A third alien appears out of nowhere, tackling a horse and rider -- the battle is not going well.

Dolarhyde and Nat pull next to each other after their first wave of attacks, two leaders taking stock of the battle:

> NAT COLORADO
> They're not going down --

> DOLARHYDE
> They will -- just keep at it.

EXT. ROCKS ABOVE SLOT CANYON - APACHES

The Apache raise their weapons -- Black Knife orders his warriors to fire and launch arrows to cover the cavalry below.

The aliens are hit, but none of them go down, the Apache salvo seemingly useless from this distance. The following exchange in Apache:

> APACHE WARRIOR
> No good. We are not hurting them. Should
> we join the fight?

Black Knife weighs the fate of his tribe and his trust of the men engaged in the battle below --

> BLACK KNIFE
> (shakes his head)
> -- hold your position -- keep firing.

EXT. EMMETT'S RIDGE - DAY

Emmett watches the battle through the telescope -- Dolarhyde moving in from one side of the terrain, and Nat charging in from the other. He continues to watch as the battle unfolds.

EXT. SLOT CANYON - CAVERN ENTRANCE - JAKE AND ELLA

Jake and Ella move toward the cavern opening -- STOP -- they see FIVE ALIENS moving toward the battlefield from the

cavern entrance. Jake and Ella tuck into a space in the
rocks to avoid being detected by the aliens as they pass.

Once the aliens are out of sight, Jake and Ella head to the
entrance, BUT TWO MORE ALIENS APPEAR -- Jake blasts them
both in a flash before either can get the drop on Jake.

They enter the cavern . . .

EXT. ROCKS ABOVE SLOT CANYON - APACHE POSITION

ANGLE ON A PAIR of Apache, away from Black Knife, taking
aim and from their perch in the rocks. They spot an alien
climbing up toward their position. The two braves retrain
their weapons on this new target, but it's TOO LATE --

-- they're ambushed by another alien already upon them.

EXT. BATTLEFIELD - DAY

Various shots: BATTLEFIELD CHAOS -- FAST

Hunt, Bronc, Bull, and Red are pinned by alien fire behind
a berm --

ANOTHER ANGLE: DOC FINISHES TYING OFF A WOUNDED MAN as the
ground EXPLODES around them --

                        DOC
         I stopped the bleeding! Now take cover!

Doc picks up Meacham's rifle -- disappears into the brush.

INT. CAVERN TUNNELS - DAY

   -- deep into the earth's bowels, they move along at a
stealth creep. As they move further, an EERIE GLOW OF
ARTIFICIAL LIGHT illuminates the corridors ahead.

INT. CAVERN TUNNELS - DAY

MEMORY FLASHCUT! Running -- escaping -- the SAME LIGHT --

BACK TO JAKE -- cuts toward it, memory guiding him:

INT. CAVERN - DAY

JAKE

This way . . .

Steam and dry heat. Jake, Ella, and the Apaches turn a corner to see OUR ABDUCTEES DANGLING FROM THE CEILING BY BOLOS, LIKE MEAT IN A BUTCHER SHOP: MARIA, PERCY, TAGGART, DEPUTY LYLE, more people from Absolution, as well as APACHE INDIANS. Staring up, catatonic, at some kind of GOOEY, DRIPPING ALIEN LIGHT SOURCE overhead that FLASHES a strobe effect -- keeping the prisoners ZOMBIFIED.

ON JAKE -- Remembering that light from his memories.

ELLA draws her pistol and SHOOTS the zombie lights. THEY EXPLODE, PHOSPHOROUS GOO raining down --

ON THE ABDUCTEES. Instantly, it's like a CIRCUIT has broken in their minds -- slowly waking from a dream -- Jake moves to Taggart --

JAKE (CONT'D)

Sheriff?

But the abductees don't recognize them yet --

JAKE (CONT'D)

How long they gonna be like this?

ELLA

-- each is different.

They suddenly come under fire from a PAIR OF ALIENS --

JAKE

(to Ella)

Go! I'll hold them off --

Ella leads the townspeople back out the way they came as Jake covers them -- returns blaster fire.

EXT. ALIEN SHIP - BATTLEFIELD - DAY

EXPLOSIONS shred the battlefield. Dolarhyde gallops through the fray as men drop:

                          DOLARHYDE
          CHARGE THE LEFT FLANK! REAR RANK, CLOSE
          UP!!!

BUT AN ALIEN LEAPS, SLAMMING SIDEWAYS INTO DOLARHYDE'S
HORSE.

Dolarhyde goes DOWN with the animal, scrambles back as
the alien LEAPS AGAIN, stabbing its lethal claw into the
ground --

COLORADO JUMPS off his horse with a WAR CRY, swinging his
club, BASHING IT INTO THE ALIEN'S SKULL just before it can
kill Dolarhyde --

The alien SCREECHES and whirls on Colorado, BITING HIM IN
THE NECK/SHOULDER -- Nat SCREAMS in pain --

DOLARHYDE EMPTIES his gun at the alien -- PEPPERING the
creature with bullets, hurting it, but it still won't go
down. The alien makes a final move toward him, then --

BLAM! A RIFLE SHOT SHATTERS THE ALIEN'S LEFT EYE -- A
direct hit through a vulnerable spot -- the alien finally
succumbs to the group assault and falls, dead at last.

Dolarhyde looks up at the source of the shot:

DOC -- perched on the ROCKS ABOVE, Meacham's rifle raised
in his hands with perfect surgical steadiness.

                            DOC
                  (looking up at the sky)
            Thank you for the steady hand, Preacher.

BACK TO DOLARHYDE -- A sigh of relief before:

                        DOLARHYDE
                Doc, get down here!

Dolarhyde races to Colorado, who's BLEEDING OUT:

Dolarhyde reaches Colorado, taking off his coat to stop
the bleeding.

                         DOLARHYDE

          Come on, Boy -- easy now, easy -- don't
          move --

Dolarhyde SCANS the wound -- desperately struggles to
staunch Colorado's blood. A look of fury and heartbreak
that says he won't accept what he sees -- Dolarhyde keeps
applying pressure to Colorado's wound in a desperate
struggle to keep him alive, but Colorado gurgles blood.
Dolarhyde knows this is it. Cradles his head . . .

                      NAT COLORADO
          Did we get one?

Dolarhyde's eyes fill with a kind of pain we haven't seen
before. REGRET for a thousand things unsaid. He forces a
weak smile:

                         DOLARHYDE
          Yeah. We got one.
                    (beat)
          DOC!

                      NAT COLORADO
          How bad is it?

                         DOLARHYDE
          It's okay . . . I'm here with you.

But this brings Dolarhyde right to the edge.

                      NAT COLORADO
          I always dreamed of riding into battle
          with you.

Finally, and only in the young man's dying moment:

                         DOLARHYDE
          I always dreamed of having a son like
          you.

Through his shock, Colorado can't believe he heard those
words. Dolarhyde takes Colorado's hand. And holds it. Eyes

COWBOYS & ALIENS I

138

locked. And that gives Colorado peace. This connection is all he ever really wanted.

> NAT COLORADO
>
> Go . . . get Percy . . .

Nat Colorado dies.

ON DOLARHYDE -- Paralyzed, heart shredded. All SOUND goes nearly SILENT -- ECHOEY REVERB.

Doc arrives too late to do anything. His face falls; sharing Dolarhyde's pain is the only tonic he can offer the man. Now Dolarhyde turns, sensing a presence:

BLACK KNIFE has witnessed this tragedy. It's brought him onto the battlefield, ready to lead his warriors alongside Dolarhyde and his men. Black Knife gestures, raising his upturned palm to the sky to mark Nat's passing to another realm. He then hands Dolarhyde a RIFLE:

And now there's something else on Dolarhyde's face: <u>RESOLVE</u>.

INT. ALIEN CAVERNS - DAY

Ella leads the townspeople to within sight of a cavern entrance leading back out into the light --

> ELLA
>
> We have to keep going.

Taggart looks at her, a trace of recognition crossing his face.

> SHERIFF TAGGART
>
> Do I know you?

> ELLA
>
> Yes, Sheriff, you know me. Emmett is waiting for you -- your grandson.

> SHERIFF TAGGART
> (striking a chord)
> Emmett -- where's Emmett?

                              ELLA

               You have to get everyone out to the
               light, do you understand?

Taggart nods -- his sense returning to him.

INT. ALIEN CAVERN - DAY

Jake finishes off the two aliens as the fight pushes him
into a MASSIVE CAVERN. Jake looks up, in awe:

THE BOTTOM OF THE ALIEN SHIP JUTS DOWN FROM THE CAVERN
CEILING. Jake reacts to the massive ship. Ella suddenly
appears next to him --

                              JAKE

               What the hell are you doing back here?

                              ELLA

               When they realize what's going on, they'll
               pull up anchor and leave. We won't be
               able to hold them long.

She quickly takes off her gun belt, gives it to him:

                         ELLA (CONT'D)

               I need the bracelet. Take it off.

                              JAKE

               What for?

                              ELLA

               I think I can use it to stop the ship
               from leaving.

He cinches on the gun, confused --

                              JAKE

               I can't get it off.

                              ELLA

               Yes you can.

                              JAKE

               How?

                              ELLA

          Same way you shoot it, with your mind.

He looks at the bracelet, frustration growing --

                              JAKE

          I can't.

She stares -- in the moment's frenzy, almost-ethereal calm:

                              ELLA

          Stop thinking. Look at me.

They LOCK EYES --

                         ELLA (CONT'D)
          I told you, stop thinking.

                              JAKE

          I'm not thinking!

As they stare into each other, a pregnant anything-could-
happen beat and then . . . it does: Jake kisses Ella. This
time, for real. Knee-quaking, passion-filled. And --

POP: The bracelet unlocks, dropping off his wrist. Uncoils
like a bandolier strap. Ella picks it up, starts pressing
the divots --

A series of FLASHING LIGHTS begins on the bracelet, a slow-
building ENERGY WHINE that suggests a COUNTDOWN SEQUENCE:

                              ELLA

          I have to go inside -- it's the only way
          --

                              JAKE

          I'm coming with you --

                              ELLA

          No.

And they LOCK EYES -- in this moment, Jake understands what
she means:

ELLA (CONT'D)

This isn't my home, Jake. It isn't my
destiny to stay.

JAKE

I'm not letting you go up there alo --

-- **BA-BLAM**! A LASER BLAST DETONATES inches from them,
forcing them to DUCK behind rocks. More lasers PING around
them, pinning them there. Through the gunfire, Jake manages
to peer out, weapon ready, to see --

THREE ALIENS lumbering forward through steam across the
cavern, firing from wrist blasters. Jake sees their LEADER:

IT HAS A RED SCAR. Jake's eyes SNAP to Ella -- a tense,
impossible moment of choice. And she says:

ELLA

You are a good man.

With that, she RUNS OFF into darkness --

JAKE

NO!!!

But Red Scar FIRES at her, forcing Jake to FIRE BACK and
give her cover -- he vaults the rocks, one hand SLAPPING
the hammer in a perfect five-shot run:

The first hits Red Scar in the neck -- it SCREECHES,
stumbles back. Two more perfect shots into the second
creature's eyes, BLINDING IT; two more into the third
alien's temple.

ON RED SCAR as it retreats into the steam, the monster
LOCKS EYES with Jake. Then, gone.

Jake snaps his barrel open, dumping bullets, slipping five
more into the chamber -- MOVES right up to the blinded
creature as it spasms on the ground -- **BLAM**! Kill shot to
the temple. Stalks on without pause, after the other two.

One thing's certain: Jake Lonergan's the deadliest gun
that ever lived. And now . . . the hunters are becoming
the hunted.

SC 111

Jake & Ella descend

WIDE

X's on
prisoners
- we see
Maria
Percy &
Taggart

Sc 113 cont'd

contd

Jake
blast
'hypno
-lite'

BOOM DWN

they,
untie
prisoners

INT. CAVERN - BELLY OF THE SHIP - CONTINUOUS

Ella has climbed the side of the ship to a DARK OPENING. She slips in, disappearing inside the ship with the DETONATOR . . .

EXT. BATTLEFIELD - DAY

Black Knife mounts up again to join the battle. He leads a charge against an approaching alien.

The alien whirls to fire at Black Knife, seemingly about to kill him, but SUDDENLY:

DOLARHYDE, on horseback, RAMS THE ALIEN FROM BEHIND! All three go flying in the rough.

As the alien moves to get up and turns his attention toward Dolarhyde, Black Knife finally reaches the alien and SPEARS HIS BLASTER CLAW INTO THE GROUND, saving Dolarhyde in return.

Almost simultaneously, as the alien reels to free his claw, A SPEAR PIERCES HIS CHEST -- reveal DOLARHYDE behind the alien, holding the spear he picked off the ground. The alien slumps dead. Dolarhyde and Black Knife share a look, realizing these things can be defeated. The others who have witnessed this get the message, too. They have to work together.

EXT. BATTLEFIELD - DAY

With Hunt, Bronc, Red, and Bull:

Bull gets an idea: He ties a piece of dynamite to his knife, lights the fuse, and charges an alien -- he leaps onto his back and stabs the knife into him -- a beat or two before **BOOOOM!** Bull and the alien vanish in a huge explosion.

EXT. RIDGE ABOVE BATTLEFIELD - CONTINUOUS

As Emmett watches the battle royale unfold below, the dog starts SNARLING: one of the ALIENS is approaching, searching:

EMMETT
(urgent whisper)

Quiet!!

But the alien SEES Emmett and FIRES -- a boulder near Emmett explodes as he and the dog scatter in different directions.

Emmett LEAPS off the ridge -- moves quickly down into a small hiding place within the twisting rocks. A quiet beat -- did he lose the alien?

Emmett GASPS as the alien appears in front of him, jaws snapping -- but too big to fit into the small space where Emmett has crawled.

The creature's secondary arms begin to unfold again to reach for Emmett, but he's been here before, and this time, the fear turns to anger. Emmett screams as his hands do something we can't see.

ANOTHER ANGLE -- surprisingly, the alien DROPS to its knees and TUMBLES OVER. Emmett rolls off -- to reveal . . .

THE BOWIE KNIFE DOLARHYDE GAVE HIM IS PLUNGED INTO THE CAVITY WHERE THE ALIEN'S SECONDARY ARMS unfold -- a weak spot with a direct line to vital organs. Emmett gasps, falls to a stunned sit. The dog finds him now, licking his face as --

EXT. BATTLEFIELD - ANOTHER PART OF THE BATTLE - DAY

The humans are GAINING GROUND. We see three Apaches taking on a single alien, led by Black Knife -- the first is BLASTED off his horse -- the second leaps onto the creature's back, SLAMMING a war club into its SKULL -- as it FALLS, Black Knife thrusts a LANCE through its hide like a toreador into a bull.

The aliens begin to hurtle back in DISORDER.

A CRY OF VICTORY!!!

DOC pulls his pistol, cocks it as moves toward a wounded alien writhing on the ground --

> DOC
>
> Hold on, I wanted to give you something before you go --
> (BLAM! BLAM!)
> Don't worry, plenty more where that came from --

BLAM! BLAM! Finally, the alien is dead.

> DOC (CONT'D)
>
> I got a perfect spot on my wall for your . . .
> (looking at its hideous face)
> I'll bet you're probably handsome for your kind, huh?

The ship begins to BUZZ eerily, preparing for departure.

INT. ALIEN SHIP - CONTINUOUS

ON ELLA, reacting as the harmonic whine of the ship's engine begins a SLOW BUILD. It's getting ready to leave. She scrambles ever forward, closing in on that BRILLIANT LIGHT SOURCE . . .

EXT. BATTLEFIELD - DAY

Dolarhyde moves to his horse, mounts up, turns toward the slot canyon --

EXT. ROCKS ABOVE BATTLEFIELD - DAY

Emmett is back in their old scouting position, sees THE ABDUCTEES moving down a secondary slot in the canyon -- among them, TAGGART, PERCY, MARIA, and LYLE.

EXT. SLOT CANYON ENTRANCE - DAY

Dolarhyde rides into the mouth of the slot canyon, dismounts as he nears the cavern entrance --

                 I see them!

Dolarhyde looks up to see Emmett waving his arms, the
signal that everyone made it out of the caverns.

                      EMMETT (CONT'D)
                 They went around the other side!

                          DOLARHYDE
                 Percy?

                          EMMETT
                 Yeah!

                          DOLARHYDE
                 What about Jake -- and Ella?

Emmett scans the crowd with his telescope -- turns back:

                          EMMETT
                 No!

INT. CAVERNS - CONTINUOUS

In the dark of the caverns, we MOVE with the WOUNDED ALIEN
that Jake shot in the temple, orange blood OOZING down its
skull . . . GASPING desperately for breath, searching . . .
as . . .

JAKE APPEARS BEHIND IT, GUN AIMED -- **BLAM!** The creature's
BLASTED AWAY. Jake creeps on, hunting Red Scar . . .

INT. ALIEN SHIP - CONTINUOUS

We are INSIDE a crawlspace on the ship, what may be the
most claustrophobic tube imaginable. The walls seem to be
made of thick gelatin, like a rubber cocoon, through which
. . .

ELLA appears, fighting her way through the shroud, hands
tearing away at the gelatin walls toward some kind of LIGHT
SOURCE in the distance . . .

THE BRACELET DETONATOR -- its alien countdown light sequence
TICKS FASTER --

INT. CAVERNS - CONTINUOUS

Jake stalks around a corner . . . and FREEZES. Because there
before him are two OPERATING TABLES. Where he escaped from:

INT. CAVERN - FLASHBACK

*FLASHBACK HITS! Jake being strapped down -- sees the alien
rolling Alice's dead body off the table -- Jake grabs the
blaster and shoots, giving Red Scar his scar --*

INT. CAVERNS - CONTINUOUS

ON JAKE -- GUT STRUCK. Nervous system almost paralyzed with
sense-memory horror.

SUDDENLY: A TALONED ARM SPEARS THROUGH HIS SHOULDER, LIFTING
HIM OFF THE GROUND. RED SCAR.

Jake SCREAMS as the alien HURTLES him across the cavern.
He SLAMS into the wall. His gun skitters off . . .

ON JAKE -- dazed, blinking -- as with incredible strength,
Red Scar GRABS him by the leg and starts DRAGGING HIM
across the cavern -- Jake's arms lash wildly, finding no
purchase --

And then he's LIFTED off the ground -- what's happening?!
-- Red Scar SLAMS him down . . .

BACK ON THE OPERATING TABLE. Jake -- and we -- are reliving
the horror all over again. Red Scar's massive taloned arms
PIN Jake's arms to the slab. The evil creature LOOMS over
Jake . . . enjoying this.

Its chest OPENS UP, and those smaller PINCER ARMS fold out,
probing at Jake. He struggles, but the alien's impossibly
stronger. One of the pincers readies a LASER CUTTER and
lowers it to Jake's face, about to finish the job . . .

                    A VOICE
        HEY.

Red Scar's head snaps up, coming face-to-barrel with:

DOLARHYDE. RIFLE RAISED: **BLAM!** Red Scar's BLASTED. Screeches, staggering -- wounded, but NOT DEAD. In a fury, Red Scar WHACKS DOLARHYDE ACROSS THE CAVERN, hard as hell, the rifle goes flying out of his hands. The alien turns now toward Dolarhyde, moments from killing him -- until:

BLAMBLAMBLAM! Jake's picked up the rifle -- UNLOADS into the alien, **BLAM! BLAM!** -- knocks him backward into --

ONE OF THE GOLD-MINING PITS. Molten gold CONSUMES RED SCAR IN A HISSING WAVEFRONT OF FLAME. The alien ignites like a match head -- staggers, shrieking, body on fire, as the gold overtakes his body . . . finally leaving only a small, uncovered trail that outlines the SCAR on his now-dead face.

Jake stands over the dying alien . . .

> JAKE
> . . . Go back to hell . . .

INT. CAVERNS - CONTINUOUS

The caverns TREMBLE, unstable now as the ship continues its departure process. Jake helps Dolarhyde off the ground --

> DOLARHYDE
> We gotta move --

> JAKE
> Not without Ella --

> DOLARHYDE
> JAKE: WE'RE OUTTA TIME.

ROCKS are falling all around them. Jake -- impossible moment of CHOICE -- Dolarhyde literally DRAGS JAKE OUT -- THEY RUN.

EXT. BATTLEFIELD - CONTINUOUS

The humans SPRINT AWAY on foot and horseback as the ground SHAKES at an earthquake richter --

The ship starts RISING UP from the ground as its thrusters
FIRE:

INT. CAVERNS TUNNELS - CONTINUOUS

JAKE AND DOLARHYDE FEEL IT FIRST -- then SEE IT COMING --
FLAME races through the caverns behind them -- RUN FASTER
-- toward the opening ahead -- at the last second they
RACE OUT and:

EXT. CAVERN ENTRANCE - CONTINUOUS

-- LEAP from the cavern opening as the EXPLOSION ROARS
OUT THE TUNNEL INTO OPEN AIR. We lose them in the blast --

EXT. SKY OVER BATTLEFIELD - CONTINUOUS

The ship EMERGES from the ground and streaks upward into
the sky . . . UP, UP, UP . . . all eyes watch, agape: NO!!!!

INT. ALIEN SHIP - CONTINUOUS

ELLA has fought her way to the ship's center -- in front
of her, the ENGINE CORE, the source of the brilliant light.

THE BRACELET DETONATOR -- its countdown sequence ZEROES
OUT:

Ella TOSSES it into the light as she's CONSUMED and FRAME
GOES WHITE:

EXT. BATTLEFIELD - CONTINUOUS

KA-BOOOOOM!!! The ship EXPLODES MIDAIR, HUGE FIREBALLS erupt
within it! The immense surge grows outward!

The mammoth fireball finally DISSIPATES over the field
. . .

The frame is WHITE with dust and SUNSHINE.

And we HOLD in this forever, as something begins to RAIN
DOWN. Looks at first like glitter . . .

GOLD DUST. When the haze starts to clear, we reveal:

OUR HERO SHOT: From the smoke, Jake and Dolarhyde emerge, walking side-by-side . . .

From the other end of the field comes the small Apache war party, leading our HUMAN SURVIVORS.

THE TOWNSFOLK OF ABSOLUTION AND THE APACHES FIND EACH OTHER. Families, lovers, friends . . . reunited.

ON DOC -- As he sees his BELOVED MARIA, stumbling weakly toward him as tears run down her cheeks. He EMBRACES her madly, kissing every inch of her face as . . .

EMMETT pushes through the crowd, sees SHERIFF TAGGART --

                    EMMETT
          GRANDPA!!!!

The kid rushes to his Grandfather, who stares back in a daze:

                 EMMETT (CONT'D)
          You're alive! It's me!!!

Some tremor of recognition flickers in Taggart -- he blinks -- Emmett smiles, gently:

                 EMMETT (CONT'D)
               (takes his grandfather's hand)
          My turn to look out for you.

Taggart looks down at his hand in the boy's. Not fully comprehending yet . . . but somehow . . . accepting.

DOLARHYDE sees BLACK KNIFE. They face each other . . . then the chief offers an arm in friendship. Dolarhyde, after a moment, grips it. Sees something over the chief's shoulder:

PERCY, stumbling forward searchingly. Dolarhyde moves to him. Percy just stares at his father's face, knows he knows it somehow . . .

                    DOLARHYDE
          You remember me, Boy?

Percy just blinks. Dolarhyde wells with emotion, though contained . . .

                    DOLARHYDE (CONT'D)
          I'm your father.

And Percy . . . SMILES. The vaguest smiles of recognition. Sweet, and somehow innocent.

                        PERCY
          Pa? I don't remember anything?

Dolarhyde takes him by the arm, gently:

                      DOLARHYDE
          Then we'll JUST have to start over.

ON JAKE, looking up at the sky, the still-dissipating explosion cloud. Ella was on that ship. His face full of loss . . . LONGING . . . and we RISE UP over the sea of bodies, until Jake's just a small figure in the crowd . . .

DISSOLVE TO:

EXT. ABSOLUTION - MAIN DRAG - DAY

   . . . HIGH AND WIDE over Absolution, now in a state of REBIRTH. Streets alive with wagons, horses, and people; tents pitched on the outskirts. Newcomers arriving, old regulars thriving. The influx of gold has turned our sleepy little hamlet into a newly thriving mecca . . .

INT. GOLD LEAF SALOON - DAY

Close on PIANO KEYS as deft hands play a version of "Lorena" for patrons, some DANCING, including MARIA AND DOC -- others laughing and drinking. The bar's HOPPING.

ANGLE - A BAG OF GOLD NUGGETS is dropped on the counter. REVEAL BRONC and HUNT, looking up at DOC as he dances:

                        HUNT
          How many more songs we gotta sit through
          before we can get a drink?

DOC

Simmer down, Hot Sauce -- just happy to
see my wife -- I'm coming.

Before he breaks away, Maria pecks him with a HOT KISS, he
grins -- Doc hurries behind the bar, grabs a bottle, and
pours Hunt and Bronc another round.

BRONC

Muy amable.

Now we notice <u>Percy</u>, sitting next to Emmett:

PERCY

A drink for me and my friend.

DOC

Isn't your friend a little young to be
sitting at the bar?

PERCY

Not after what he's been through. Two
sarsaparillas.
    (beat, handing over some bills)
And this should take care of any
outstanding debts, and I thank you for
your patience.

Percy is, indeed, a new man. Doc grins in appreciation,
serves them gladly. Emmett beams at being treated like one
of the boys.

ANOTHER ANGLE -- saloon doors swing open -- DOLARHYDE
ENTERS, a ledger under his arm:

DOLARHYDE

Percy.

The piano music stops -- all eyes on Dolarhyde . . .

PERCY

Coming, Pa.

Percy stands, moves to Dolarhyde -- everyone waiting to see what happens next. Dolarhyde surveys the patrons -- finally:

                    DOLARHYDE
          Next round's on the Dolarhydes.

A cheer rises. Piano music starts again as Dolarhyde and Percy step outside.

EXT. ABSOLUTION - MAIN STREET - DAY

ANGLE - TRACKING - DOLARHYDE AND PERCY

As they walk through town now, passing citizens who nod and tip their hats -- GRATITUDE in their eyes. Dolarhyde nods back as he talks to Percy, mentoring him:

                    DOLARHYDE
               Real soon, people're gonna be hearing
               about the gold. Won't be long before
               there's a railroad spur in here -- gonna
               change the entire nature of the business.
               People who make money'll be feeding
               cattle, not running 'em --
                    (beat)
               Get these ledgers to the bank, tell him I
               need some new checks printed up.

Percy stops.

                    DOLARHYDE (CONT'D)
                    (taken aback)
               Tell him I want them to read, Dolarhyde
               and Son.
                    (beat)
               That okay with you?

Dolarhyde looks at his boy. For the first time, a better father:

And Percy grins. For the first time, a better son:

                    PERCY
          Yes. Yes, Sir.

Percy moves off as Dolarhyde approaches the SHERIFF'S OFFICE. Find Taggart on a chair with his feet up on a railing, the dog by his side:

> **DOLARHYDE**
> (a nod)
> John.

> **SHERIFF TAGGART**
> Woodrow. Our town's about to get a whole lot bigger.

> **DOLARHYDE**
> Hope that won't be a problem for you, Sheriff. This is your town -- and if it wasn't before, it sure is now.

ANGLE ON -- Jake rides up. Stops in front of everyone on the porch. Dolarhyde steps forward to greet him.

> **DOLARHYDE (CONT'D)**
> You were gonna leave without saying goodbye?

> **JAKE**
> Still a wanted man.

> **DOLARHYDE**
> I could swear I saw Jake Lonergan die in those caves.
> (turns to . . .)
> Isn't that right, Sheriff?

> **SHERIFF TAGGART**
> Damn shame we couldn't hang him ourselves.

> **DOLARHYDE**
> (a beat)
> Man has a right to start fresh. And I got my gold back.

> **JAKE**
> That what you're doing? Get a rocking chair, sit out front while someone polishes your boots?

DOLARHYDE

You want the job?

Jake grins. Slips on his hat.

                    DOLARHYDE (CONT'D)
I could always use a gun like you around.

                         JAKE
Yes, you could.

Now, Dolarhyde grins too.

                       DOLARHYDE
Jake.
          (Jake stops; turns back)
She's in a better place.
          (alt:)
Take care of yourself.

The men lock eyes. Bonded in loss. Bonded in new beginnings.
Finally, Jake tips his hat:

                         JAKE
Be seeing you round.
          (beat)
Colonel.

Dolarhyde takes that. Tips his hat in return. And watches
Jake ride out of town. As MUSIC takes us to . . .

EXT. ABANDONED CABIN - DAY

FLOWERS are set down on the porch. Jake lowers himself to
a knee. Eyes CLOSE. And we PUSH IN, slowly . . . until his
eyes FILL FRAME. HOLD . . . then, the barest WHISPER on
the wind . . .

                      ELLA (V.O.)
 . . . Jake . . .

His eyes OPEN. He turns. Nothing . . .

A FLUTTERING sound. We finally reveal the source . . .

A HUMMING BIRD is dancing toward him in the wind. He watches it hover right in front of him, almost playful . . .

ON JAKE -- A thousand emotions swirl in his eyes. In this moment, we sense he makes a pivotal transition. Receives this as a message. Of hope. Possibility. He looks around. And just barely . . . grins:

SMASH CUT TO:

Jake RIDING AWAY from the cabin, toward the setting sun . . .

ANOTHER ANGLE: Looking down on the canyon from a cliff above, we see Jake riding away into the future . . . as we TRACK TO:

THE FIGURE OF A WOMAN ON THE CLIFF, her back to us. Haloed by the brilliant sun.

We don't see her face. We don't need to. AS MUSIC SWELLS:

FADE OUT.

T H E   E N D

About the Screenwriters

RTO ORCI and **ALEX KURTZMAN** have been working together more than 18 years. Their TV credits include *Alias*, *nge* and *Hawaii Five-0*. Their feature film credits clude *Mission: Impossible III*, *Transformers* and *ar Trek*.

DAMON LINDELOF's credits include *Crossing Jordan* and the Golden Globe and Emmy Award-winning *Lost*. Lindelof was also a producer on J.J. Abrams' *Star Trek* reboot. He is currently writing and producing the sequel to *Star Trek*.

MARK FERGUS and **HAWK OSTBY** co-wrote the blockbuster *Iron Man* and were nominated for an Academy Award® for their work on the film *Children of Men*.

STEVE OEDEKERK, the Academy Award®-nominated and Emmy Award-winning multi-hyphenate, has experienced much success in writing, directing, producing, acting, stand-up comedy and computer-generated animation.

COWBOYS & ALIENS™

THE ILLUSTRATED SCREENPLAY

1875. New Mexico Territory. A stranger with no memory of his past stumbles into the hard desert town of Absolution. The only hint to his history is a mysterious shackle that encircles one of his wrists. What he discovers is that the people of Absolution don't welcome strangers, and nobody makes a move on its streets unless ordered to do so by the iron-fisted Colonel Dolarhyde. It's a town that lives in fear.

But Absolution is about to experience fear it can scarcely comprehend as the desolate city is attacked by marauders from the sky. Screaming down with breathtaking velocity and blinding lights to abduct the helpless one by one, these monsters challenge everything the residents have ever known.

Now, the stranger they rejected is their only hope for salvation. As this gunslinger slowly starts to remember who he is and where he's been, he realizes he holds a secret that could give the town a fighting chance against the alien force. With the help of the elusive traveler Ella, he pulls together a posse comprised of former opponents—townsfolk, Dolarhyde and his boys, outlaws, and Apache warriors—all in danger of annihilation. United against a common enemy, they prepare for an epic showdown for survival.

INCLUDES

- **The shooting script**
- **Concept art**
- **Storyboard art**

PLUS: Unit photography featuring Daniel Craig, Harrison Ford, Olivia Wilde, Sam Rockwell, Adam Beach, Paul Dano, and Noah Ringer

ABOUT THE SCREENPLAY

Screenplay by Roberto Orci & Alex Kurtzman & Damon Lindelof and Mark Fergus & Hawk Ostby. Screen Story by Mark Fergus & Hawk Ostby and Steve Oedekerk. Based on Platinum Studios' "Cowboys and Aliens" by Scott Mitchell Rosenberg.

UNIVERSAL PICTURES / DREAMWORKS PICTURES / RELIANCE BIG ENTERTAINMENT PRESENT IN ASSOCIATION WITH RELATIVITY MEDIA AN IMAGINE ENTERTAINMENT / K/O PAPER PRODUCTS / FAIRVIEW ENTERTAINMENT / PLATINUM STUDIOS PRODUCTION A JON FAVREAU FILM DANIEL CRAIG HARRISON FORD "COWBOYS & ALIENS" OLIVIA WILDE SAM ROCKWELL ADAM BEACH PAUL DANO NOAH RINGER MUSIC BY HARRY GREGSON-WILLIAMS COSTUME DESIGNER MARY ZOPHRES EDITED BY DAN LEBENTAL ACE PRODUCTION DESIGNER SCOTT CHAMBLISS DIRECTOR OF PHOTOGRAPHY MATTHEW LIBATIQUE ASC EXECUTIVE PRODUCERS STEVEN SPIELBERG JON FAVREAU DENIS L. STEWART BOBBY COHEN RANDY GREENBERG RYAN KAVANAUGH PRODUCED BY BRIAN GRAZER RON HOWARD ALEX KURTZMAN ROBERTO ORCI SCOTT MITCHELL ROSENBERG BASED ON PLATINUM STUDIOS' "COWBOYS AND ALIENS" BY SCOTT MITCHELL ROSENBERG SCREEN STORY BY MARK FERGUS & HAWK OSTBY AND STEVE OEDEKERK
DREAMWORKS PICTURES THIS FILM IS NOT YET RATED VISUAL EFFECTS AND ANIMATION BY INDUSTRIAL LIGHT & MAGIC SCREENPLAY BY ROBERTO ORCI & ALEX KURTZMAN & DAMON LINDELOF AND MARK FERGUS & HAWK OSTBY DIRECTED BY JON FAVREAU A UNIVERSAL PICTURE UNIVERSAL
© 2010 UNIVERSAL STUDIOS AND DREAMWORKS II DISTRIBUTION CO., LLC
www.cowboysandaliensmovie.com

INSIGHT EDITIONS
P.O. Box 3088
San Rafael, CA 94912
www.insighteditions.com

© 2011 Universal Studios and DreamWorks II Dist. Cowboys & Aliens ™ & © Universal Studios and DreamWorks II Dist. Licensed by Universal Studios Licensing LLC. All Rights Reserved.

ISBN 978-1-60887-025-7 • US $18.95
51895
9 781608 870257